"Janet Denison is a contagious perso⟨ ⟩ teacher, and refreshingly transparent. ⟨ ⟩ little deeper, to think and question a⟨ ⟩ll-ness and silence. This book carries th⟨ ⟩l-grimage that Janet embraces with her whole heart, the pilgrimage of being remade into the likeness of Christ."

VERDELL DAVIS KRISHER, One Hope Ministries
Author of *Let Me Grieve, But Not Forever*

"This book is a must-read for the countless Christians who have filled their calendars with ministry but have fallen away from their personal walk with God. Janet Denison blends touching accounts from her own experience with clear direction from Scripture in a masterful way, pointing each of us to a higher calling than Christian service alone can provide. The invitation for Christians to step off the 'spiritual treadmill' and truly walk with God could not have come at a more perfect time."

DR. GARY COOK, President, Dallas Baptist University

"Janet Denison shares my heart for the revival of God's people. I pray God will use her words to compel you to refuse to settle for less than a godly life . . . from His perspective."

ANNE GRAHAM LOTZ, International speaker
Author of *Just Give Me Jesus* and *I Saw the LORD*

"With wisdom gained from her own personal pursuit of godliness, Janet Denison writes passionately about living for God things, not just good things. Janet's style is warm and practical as she teaches us that godliness is firmly based on God's Word and consists of living wisely, humbly, and simply. After studying the key Scriptures in each chapter and reading Janet's thoughts, I was blessed and challenged by her excellent reminder that true contentment can only be found in God's call to be godly."

CYNTHIA HEALD, Navigators
Author of *Maybe God Is Right After All* and *Uncommon Beauty*

CONTENT TO BE GOOD,

CALLED TO BE GODLY

JANET DENISON

Tyndale House Publishers, Inc.
Carol Stream, Illinois

Visit Tyndale's exciting Web site at www.tyndale.com

Visit Janet Denison's Web site at soulworkministries.com

TYNDALE and Tyndale's quill logo are registered trademarks of Tyndale House Publishers, Inc.

Content to Be Good, Called to Be Godly: What to Do When Your Life Is Full, but Your Soul Is Empty

Designed by Beth Sparkman

Edited by Bonne L. Steffen

Published in association with Rosenbaum & Associates Literary Agency, Brentwood, Tennessee.

Library of Congress Cataloging-in-Publication Data

Denison, Janet.
  Content to be good, called to be godly : what to do when your life is full, but your soul is empty / Janet Denison.
    p. cm.
  ISBN-13: 978-1-4143-1615-4 (sc)
  ISBN-10: 1-4143-1615-1 (sc)
  1. Spiritual formation.   2. Denison, Janet.   I. Title.
  BV4511.D46 2008
  248.4—dc22   2008005509

Printed in the United States of America

14   13   12   11   10   09   08
 7   6   5   4   3   2   1

Contents

Acknowledgments

Thank you, Jim.
You have been my teacher, my encourager, my best friend, and a godly husband.
You are the love of my life and my greatest blessing.

Thank you, Ryan and Craig.
You have given me love and support and have been my two most important fans.
I am grateful that you listen, you care, and you walk with God.
You are my greatest joy.

Thank you, Esther sisters.
You have studied with me, caused me to think, and inspired ideas.
Most especially, you have prayed. You have been my greatest help.

Thank you, Loyd and Michal.
You provided a quiet and beautiful place where I could listen to God.

Thank you to my parents, my friends, and the churches we have served.
It really does take a village!

And thank you Bucky, Jan, and John.
I needed an opportunity and help—and you were willing to give both.
May God bless each of you in his perfect way.

Introduction

This book is written for those who have a personal relationship with God but want to walk with him on a higher level of Christian maturity. Spiritual growth can be like physical growth. Children mature naturally and rapidly. One day we are reaching down to tie a shoe and soon we find ourselves reaching up to adjust a mortarboard or wedding veil. The changes from youth to adulthood are easy to measure and natural to expect. Maturity becomes more of a choice in our adult years. The same can be true spiritually. The lessons taught in this book are for those who want to make that choice to mature in their faith. You may, like many Christians, go to church faithfully each week, attend Bible studies, and try to follow the lessons you've learned. But what if your faith becomes routine and loses the powerful joy that accompanied your salvation?

I've been there as a pastor's wife and a Bible study leader. My normal routine requires me to be involved in church activities and the preparations for them. I spend a lot of time reading the Bible and other resources so that I can teach a lesson or speak to a group. I had to learn that *using* the Bible to prepare a lesson wasn't the same thing as taking time *with* the Bible to grow personally. I was in full-time ministry but realized that I was trudging spiritually because my relationship with God had become a monotonous routine of fulfilling time commitments and meeting expectations. I knew how to give the appearance of spirituality, but I had lost the joy and power of a vital relationship with the Father. This book describes my spiritual life-lessons—lessons that may be beneficial to you, too.

Content to Be Good, Called to Be Godly is a self-contained Bible study. It can be used in small group settings or for larger group discussion. It can also be used as a tool for personal study. The book contains my thoughts, Scripture passages, and thought-provoking questions to help you examine your spiritual life and encourage you to experience the life God has called you to live. God told the prophet Jeremiah, "I know the plans *I* have for you" (Jeremiah 29:11, emphasis added). God has a plan for your life, but he created you with free will; therefore, following his plan will be a choice. This book also has an appendix with further helps. But that's just the starting point. Your spiritual journey will not change dramatically until you really dig deep into Scripture. God's Word has the power to change your life. The most important part of this book isn't what I have said, but what God will say through his Word as you study.

The reason most Christians plateau spiritually is because they have an unbalanced spiritual diet. They consume too much milk and not enough meat. It's a common fact that when a mother consumes food, her body processes it into milk. It's not that different for us who are growing spiritually. We expect to grow primarily through the "milk" of sermons, books, lectures, and lessons. A pastor, teacher, or author takes the Word of God, processes it, and gives it to the people listening. But just as milk isn't enough nourishment to sustain an adult, the same is true for our spiritual diet. The "meat" you consume will be the lessons you are taught directly, by the Holy Spirit, as you prayerfully study the Scriptures for yourself. Paul told the church in Corinth,

Dear brothers and sisters, when I was with you I couldn't talk to you as I would to spiritual people. I had to talk as though you belonged to this world or as though you were infants in the Christian life. I had to feed you with milk, not with solid food, because you weren't ready for anything stronger. **1 Corinthians 3:1-2**

This book has both milk and meat. You will need to consume both to fully benefit from each lesson. Spiritual health requires a balanced diet so that we can grow to be mature Christians, strong enough to follow God's plan.

This book was born on my morning walks. I don't walk for the rush of endorphins or because I hope to be a size four someday. I walk for the reward of ice cream, pasta, and the opportunity to think. I enjoy having quiet time to think, so I walk. For me, morning is the best time to walk. I love the way the world looks and sounds in the morning. The day is new and fresh with promise.

Every morning I pass people beginning their days—retrieving their paper from the driveway, driving to work, taking the kids to school, jogging past me. I often wonder who among the people I see are going to heaven. I'm certain many of them are Christians, but which ones will choose to walk closely with Jesus for the day?

My husband and I have served wonderful churches over the years. But at every one of those churches I see people come each Sunday simply because they know they should.

They attend worship and Bible study, then leave—believing they have met God's expectations for the week. I can recognize those who are content with being good instead of godly because I saw that person in my own mirror for a long time. When Jesus taught his disciples—including us—to pray "Give us this day our daily bread," he was saying that we need God's presence and nourishment on a daily basis.

There is a difference between finding joy in moments and being filled with the joy and peace of a solid relationship with Jesus. I pray this book will help you rediscover your passion for Jesus and reconnect with him on a deeper level. When you think of the impact the early Christians had on their society, just imagine the potential impact we could have on our world.

I don't want you just to be a good parent; I want you to be a godly one. I don't want you to know success in this world; I want you to receive a heavenly reward. I don't want you to have a good reputation; I want others to see Jesus in you. I don't want you to be content to be good; I want you to understand that you are called to be godly.

More important, I want *you* to study Scripture and listen to what God tells you through his Holy Spirit. I wrote this book for the Christian who knows there is a better way to live faithfully and desires to do so. All of us yearn to hear God say, "Well done, my good and faithful servant." The chapters of this book hopefully will teach you how to live the godly life of a faithful servant, the life we have been called to live. As you read the lessons I needed to learn (and am still learning), maybe you'll find you need to learn them too. Let's both be willing to follow our godly calling.

One

CONTENT TO BE GOOD, CALLED TO BE GODLY

Early morning has always been my favorite time of the day. I love to work in those quiet hours when most of the world is either asleep or barely getting started. For years I've risen early, grabbed a cup of hot coffee, and spent time with God. Each week I routinely set aside one morning to prepare my weekly Bible study, a teaching ministry that I have had for many years. It is my privilege to teach women of all ages and from a variety of backgrounds who come to our church. Some have a great deal of Bible knowledge, while others are just beginning to read the Scriptures. They meet together in small groups to discuss a portion of Scripture, and then I present a more in-depth look at the passage.

One beautiful fall morning several years ago, my routine changed. In the past, I had usually anticipated the chance to study, but as I headed upstairs my feet seemed heavy. I had no desire to prepare my weekly Bible lesson. We were studying the life of Christ, and the week's lesson focused on the temptations of Jesus in the desert. Here I was with one of the most well-known passages in the New Testament, and I was completely uninspired. It is always more difficult to teach a well-known passage. Most of the ladies had heard this Bible story in Vacation Bible School and had been hearing it in lessons and sermons ever since. I couldn't imagine that I would have anything new to add.

I sat in my favorite chair and carefully read through the passage, studying each verse. When I finished, I got to my knees, asking God for *something* I could say that would be new and interesting. I finished praying and looked again at the fourth chapter of Luke, hoping that I would be led to *at least* three points and a clever introduction. Still, nothing new came to mind. *Perhaps I just need more caffeine to fill in the gaps where God's silence seems to be growing,* I thought to myself. In the kitchen I poured another cup of coffee and then sat for a long time at the kitchen table looking out the window. The leaves of the oak trees were just beginning to turn, and they held the promise of the full array of fall colors. The sun poured through the windows, and the house was hushed and peaceful. Once again my mind drifted to the Scripture I had just read.

Then Jesus, full of the Holy Spirit, returned from the Jordan River. He was led by the Spirit in the wilderness, where he was tempted by the devil for forty days. Jesus ate nothing all that time and became very hungry. Then the devil said to him, "If you are the Son of God, tell this stone to become a loaf of bread." But Jesus told him, "No! The Scriptures say, 'People do not live by bread alone.'" Then the devil took him up and revealed to him all the kingdoms of the world in a moment of time. "I will give you the glory of these kingdoms and authority over them," the devil said, "because they are mine to give to anyone I please. I will give it all to you if you will worship me." Jesus replied, "The Scriptures say, 'You must worship the LORD your God and serve only him.'" Then the devil took him to Jerusalem, to the highest point of the Temple, and said, "If you are the Son of God, jump off! For the Scriptures say, 'He will order his angels to protect and guard you. And they will hold you up with their hands so you won't even hurt your foot on a stone.'" Jesus responded, "The Scriptures also say, 'You must not test the LORD your God.'" When the devil had finished tempting Jesus, he left him until the next opportunity came. **Luke 4:1-13**

As I looked again at the familiar passage, my mind filled with a steady stream of silent questions. *Why did the Spirit lead Christ into the wilderness? Was this really necessary?* God is omniscient and already knew how Christ would respond. *Why did the devil choose those temptations for Christ? Did Satan think Jesus would agree with his ideas?* I began to think about all the things Satan offered Jesus. To be honest, there didn't seem to be anything wrong with the devil's suggestions. *Why should Jesus go hungry? Why shouldn't he prove to the world that he is the Son of God?* Looking objectively at Satan's offers, they all seemed like pretty *good* ideas.

A few moments later God's Spirit began to author the quiet thoughts that answered my questions. His presence was tangible. As God gave me the lesson I had been struggling to create, I realized it was more important than an outline for a weekly Bible study lesson—it was a life lesson for me. That morning I came to realize the temptations of Christ were *not* just his. . . . They were mine as well.

It made me think: *How many times in my life has Satan presented me with offers similar to what Satan offered Christ— offers of personal gain or glory that I have willingly accepted?* In fact, I believed that these offers would result in a valuable service for God. I counted off the times I had driven home from a speaking engagement or Bible study quite proud of how things had gone. When people complimented me on how I "ministered to the crowd," I assumed God was as pleased as they were. In reality, I had been led to a temple and I had jumped.

I stared quietly at the empty, stained coffee cup in my hands, realizing that my soul was just like that cup. Yes, I had been working hard, but to what end? That morning I honestly questioned if I was busy with the Lord's agenda for my life or if I was simply caught up in the devil's suggestions. I had a ministry . . . but was it mine, or God's?

That quiet fall morning was an appointment with God. Realizing the significance of this moment, my next prayer to God was to seek his help, not just for a message to teach, but for my life. I had wanted God to help me write a lesson that was clever and new so I could impress those who came to listen. I wanted to turn stones into bread so I could feed my ego. I wanted to do a good job so that the Bible study would grow and I would look successful. I was working for those kingdoms and glories the devil had offered. I wanted to be inspired so that others would see that God had chosen me and was using my ministry. I wanted to jump from the Temple. I wanted precisely what the devil was offering, never realizing that the good things I was busy doing were much more about me than they were about God. I was paying Satan's high price as I spent my time, my energy, and my passion on his delusions; the currency required was depleting my soul. My calendar was full and I was actively doing things the world called ministry, but I was exhausted, joyless, and spiritually bankrupt. I wanted to rediscover the life God wanted me to have. The life he could bless.

God heard my prayers and answered them that beautiful fall morning. He gave me something new to say about those verses from Luke, not so I could entertain or impress an audience, but so I could learn the message myself. He led me to a new understanding of what would be necessary if I wanted to live by God's plan and for his purpose. In those early morning hours, alone with my Father, he began to teach me what would become a central message of my ministry and a passion for my own life. God called me to reorder my priorities and to ask myself if I was busy doing good things—or God things. Now he wants to ask you that same question.

❧ POINTS TO PONDER

Consider your life. What obligations involve your time and energy? How did you decide to become involved in this work? What has been your reward?

YOU WERE MADE TO BE MORE

The Holy Spirit led Jesus into the desert to be tempted. Jesus was obedient to the Spirit for the sake of his earthly ministry. His goal was to set the example for our ministries as well. Look again at the passage in Luke 4:1-13 and consider these questions.

> When did the devil choose to tempt Jesus? Why is this timing significant?

> Look at Jesus' response to each temptation. What would be the benefit of acceptance? What would be the cost of acceptance?
> - turn the stones into bread
>
> - accept glory and authority in the world
>
> - jump from the Temple and allow the angels to protect him

> Jesus came to show the world that he was the Messiah, the Son of God. How would he have accomplished his purpose by following the devil's suggestions?

Committed Christians, actively walking with the Lord, are rarely tempted to commit overt and blatant sins. For example, have you ever been tempted to rob a bank on your way to church or burn down a building before Bible study? We are children of God and we value our witness in this world. We desire the blessing of our Father. We want to be good people and good examples while living on this earth.

Satan knew Jesus wouldn't steal or murder so he would never suggest those temptations. Jesus wanted people to know that he was God's Son, so Satan tempted Jesus to fulfill that purpose . . . *apart* from God's plan. Philippians 2:6-7 says, "Though he was God, he did not think of equality with God as something to cling to. Instead, he gave up his divine privileges; he took the humble position of a slave and was born as a human being." Jesus gave up the right to plan his ministry on earth and chose instead to become a slave, obedient to his Father's plan. The devil knew he couldn't have Jesus' soul for eternity, so he made an attempt to affect Jesus' earthly ministry. Is it possible that the devil tempts Christians in much the same ways as he tempted Christ? Could this be one of the reasons the Holy Spirit led Jesus into the desert—as an illustration of how Satan tempts those who follow God?

Christians have the assurance of eternal life (John 3:16), but we live earthly lives filled with choices. Satan loves to assert his subtle, destructive influence on those choices. Satan cannot have your soul, so he will attempt to destroy your witness and limit your ability to minister.

In the temptation account, Jesus had just been baptized and was about to begin his earthly ministry. Interestingly enough, this incident is the only time in Scripture when the

Spirit of God intentionally leads someone to be tempted. Why was it necessary for Christ to be tempted? In 2 Corinthians 5:21 it says, "For God made Christ, who never sinned, to be the offering for our sin, so that we could be made right with God through Christ." Christ was tempted so that he could fulfill Old Testament prophecy and, ultimately, his earthly purpose as the perfect lamb, an offering for our sin. Jesus resisted the temptations of Satan, teaching us that we can resist them as well. He died because we wouldn't always succeed. He is our High Priest, who understands our weaknesses, "for he faced all of the same testings we do, yet he did not sin" (Hebrews 4:15). Satan hoped that Jesus would choose to show the world that he was the Messiah by proving his greatness. Jesus resisted the temptation to prove himself and chose instead to sacrifice *his* greatness and prove God's.

It's the same for us. I can stand in front of a group and teach a lesson, hoping to impress someone, or I can teach because I have yielded my mind and motives to God; then he can reach someone. Satan tempts us to believe that we are the ones who exhibit God's power because of the great things that we do for him. Scripture teaches us to show the power of God by the great things he does *through* us. Listen to Acts 1:8: "But you will receive power when the Holy Spirit comes upon you. And you will *be* my witnesses, telling people about me everywhere—in Jerusalem, throughout Judea, in Samaria, and to the ends of the earth" (emphasis added). The Greek word used for "be" is *esesthe*, meaning "to have your nature become." When the Holy Spirit came into your life, he didn't come to help you *act* like a witness for Christ. Instead, he gave you a new nature, so that you could *become* a witness. Witnessing is not something you do—it is who God re-created you to *be* when he saved you. It is your Christian purpose, and that is what the devil relentlessly attempts to destroy.

If you are a Christian, then Satan is at work in your life. Do you recognize his tactics? I didn't. As a busy preacher's wife, I spent most of my time at church. I taught Bible study and Sunday school, worked at Vacation Bible School, went to committee meetings, visited the sick in hospitals, made phone calls, counseled, prayed, and did all the other things that came with the job. People seemed grateful for what I did, so I assumed that God was equally appreciative. How could Satan be influencing my life when I was so busy doing good things *for* God? I had been acting like a Christian and trying to perform as a Christian should, but it was just that—an act and a performance.

That pivotal morning, I realized that Satan's influence was keeping me busy with good things that brought me praise rather than God things that brought God glory. I had been using vast amounts of time doing what God had never called me to do. I knew that my busy agenda had probably hindered the plan God would have designed for my life. So I made a commitment to relearn what it would mean to follow God. Will you?

❦ POINTS TO PONDER

How is Satan tempting you? It is the devil's goal to hinder you from following God's plan. What is the devil suggesting

that has the appearance of a good idea but is intended to separate you from God and his call in your life?

REPLACE GOOD IDEAS WITH GOD'S PLAN

So how can you adjust your life to God's plan and discern whether or not your choice is a good thing or a God thing? Peter addressed this problem in a letter he wrote to the Jewish Christians who had been scattered from Jerusalem. These Christians had given up everything to follow Christ, suffering persecution and loss—sometimes even of their lives—for their faith. They had established churches in other cities and were trying to share the gospel with their new neighbors. Almost immediately they discovered there would be temptations, conflict, and discord among God's people. Peter wrote to them . . . and to us:

> *So humble yourselves under the mighty power of God, and at the right time he will lift you up in honor. Give all your worries and cares to God, for he cares about you. Stay alert! Watch out for your great enemy, the devil. He prowls around like a roaring lion, looking for someone to devour. Stand firm against him, and be strong in your faith.* **1 Peter 5:6-9**

How should we "humble ourselves"? Why?

Our worries and concerns consume much of our time and energy. What does Peter suggest doing for this problem?

What is Satan "devouring" while you are clinging to your own agenda?

According to Peter, what is the solution?

We, as Christians, are often busy doing good things for God, taking satisfaction when other people seem pleased or, even better, impressed. But in the quiet moments, do you wonder why the joy and peace that God has promised is absent from your life? It is easy to assume that if the church or other Christians are pleased, then God must be pleased as well.

When these beliefs become ingrained in our minds, we grow perilously close to developing what I have described as a "treadmill ministry." Do you feel like you are running hard but never really seeing the eternal value of your efforts? Once we get on that treadmill, our service becomes routine and predictable. We get into that familiar habit of serving a church or a group of people instead of serving the Lord. It's the same, over and over again—uninspired but conventional. A Christian can spend untold hours working for others, serving the needs of others time after time. Usually those requests are well intentioned, for a program that appears to be a good idea. How do you know if you have been asked to do a good thing or called by God to a service for him?

For many years I worried that the church would be disappointed or would gossip about me if I didn't show up to almost everything on the schedule. I was the pastor's wife, and I cared what the congregation thought and said of me. I wanted their praise and honor. I wanted what Satan had tempted me to want, and I knew how to get it. I accepted almost any opportunity for ministry that looked like a good idea. I was quick to volunteer to teach a class, make a casserole, or decorate a table for a program. I was consistently reading the Bible to prepare a lesson, rather than spending time with God. I prayed the opening and closing prayers at programs, but I wasn't having very many conversations with my heavenly Father. I raced through life, filling it with good things and hoping I would impress God and others. All the while, Satan was devouring my time and my soul, one bite at a time. I spent so much time at the church, working with other Christians, that I rarely came in contact with someone outside the faith. I was running on the spiritual treadmill, and Satan was pleased because I was in the church, running in place.

Meanwhile God was saying, "Humble yourself. You only *think* you know what you should do. Let me fill you with my mighty power because you are not strong enough on your own. Work for my honor, not other people's opinions. Trust me to handle the worries and concerns. Don't you realize how much I care about you? Watch out! Satan wants to devour your time and your soul. Stand with me against the temptation to do what you or others think will be good. I will call you to your ministries, and your strength and guidance will come from trusting me. Stand firm in your faith, and I will fight the roaring lion for you."

You can be sure that Satan is hard at work, tempting God's children to be content with a life and ministry consisting of the good things that we design for ourselves. We are only a threat to him when we answer God's *call* to service, dedicated to the advancement of God's Kingdom and glory. Satan doesn't mind if people think you are good. He doesn't mind if you fill your time doing good things. In fact, the devil will try to tempt you to do exactly that. The "good person" is not the one who annoys the devil—the godly Christian poses the threat. Satan will tempt you to be good because he fears you will be godly.

Have you been tempted, as I was, to be content with a good Christian life? Are you spending your time trying to please others, or do you seek the blessing of God's approval? Do you grasp that God has called you to a higher standard? Oswald Chambers wrote, "It is not a lack of spiritual experience that leads to failure, but a lack of working to keep our eyes focused and on the right goal. . . . Is my primary goal in life to please Him and to be acceptable to Him, or is it something less, no matter how lofty it may sound?"[1]

Treadmill ministry will force you to run until you are tired and can go no further. Treadmill ministry will keep you in one place, secluded from the larger world. Treadmill ministry is our programmed effort, not a Spirit-led journey. The most dangerous consequence of a treadmill ministry is that the only person affected is the one doing the running.

Is your primary goal to please God or is it to complete programs of service designed by others? There is a higher call.

Determine to Choose the Higher Standard

How can we stay focused on the right goals? How can we be sure that the choices we make are God's leading and not the suggestions of the devil? None of us wants to fail. But we live in a world that can often demand and direct more loudly than God. We live in a society that rewards us for the good things we do but can reject us for serving God and speaking the truths of Scripture. Paul lived in a society with similar challenges. He is a great example of someone who used his life for the glory of God and resisted the temptation to work for the world's rewards. He told the church in Ephesus:

Carefully determine what pleases the Lord. Take no part in the worthless deeds of evil and darkness; instead, expose them. It is shameful even to talk about the things that ungodly people do in secret. But their evil intentions will be exposed when the light shines on them, for the light makes everything visible. This is why it is said, "Awake, O sleeper, rise up from the dead, and Christ will give you light." So be careful how you live. Don't live like fools, but like those who are wise. Make the most of every opportunity in these evil days. Don't act thoughtlessly, but understand what the Lord wants you to do. Don't be drunk with wine, because that will ruin your life. Instead, be filled with the Holy Spirit, singing psalms and hymns and spiritual songs among yourselves, and making music to the Lord in your hearts. And give thanks for everything to God the Father in the name of our Lord Jesus Christ.   **Ephesians 5:10-20**

How can you carefully determine what pleases the Lord?

Look closely at the passage. What exposes the deeds of evil and darkness?

What does Paul say we should do with the opportunities that come?

What is the opposite of acting thoughtlessly?

A person who is drunk on wine is under its control. Paul contrasts that person with one who is "filled with" or controlled by the Holy Spirit. Describe the life of a person who is under the influence of the Spirit.

POINT TO PONDER

Do you look at a chance to minister as an opportunity or an obligation?

That morning, as I stared at those trees, I knew the leaves would soon change to the glorious colors of fall because that is what God created them to do. I also knew that my life and my soul would change for the same reason.

We need to do what God *created* us to do. We are not allowed to be content filling our lives with good things we choose to do. We have a higher calling. We are called to be godly. Ephesians 5:1-2 says, "Imitate God, therefore, in everything you do, because you are his dear children. Live a life filled with love, following the example of Christ." Christ submitted his life fully to his Father, and we are to follow his example. As the children of God, we are supposed to act like our Father. We need to yield our will to God's plan and his choices. The goal is to be "carefully determined" to be involved in God things instead of good things.

I sat down at the computer that day and wrote my message. I didn't want to give it for my glory. Its success wouldn't be contingent on the listeners' approval. I would not use my spiritual gifts to bring attention to myself. Instead, I wanted to deliver a message that was authored by the Holy Spirit of God. I wanted his blessing more than the praise of others. God taught me some crucial life lessons that morning, lessons that I have struggled to remember since that time.

I had developed my own definition of Christian success rather than accepting God's word on the subject. I had worked for the immediate gratification of earthly rewards rather than waiting for the greater reward God was keeping for me in heaven. The life lessons I learned that morning redefined my life and my ministry, allowing me to step off my spiritual treadmill and walk with God. The life lessons I learned were these:

THE MEASURE OF SUCCESS

What is more pleasing to the LORD: your burnt offerings and sacrifices or your obedience to his voice? Listen! Obedience is better than sacrifice, and submission is better than offering the fat of rams.   **1 Samuel 15:22**

Success will be measured by obedience to his call.

THE ONLY REWARD OF GREAT VALUE

Because of God's grace to me, I have laid the foundation like an expert builder. Now others are building on it. But whoever is building on this foundation must be very careful. For no one can lay any foundation other than the one we already have—Jesus Christ. Anyone who builds on that foundation may use a variety of materials—gold, silver, jewels, wood, hay, or straw. But on the judgment day, fire will reveal what kind of work each builder has done. The fire will show if a person's work has any value.   **1 Corinthians 3:10-13**

This reward will be saved in heaven, not gained by the response of people.

That week I didn't teach *my* message. . . . I taught the one God gave me. That week I didn't see leading my Bible study as an obligation but as an opportunity. I said yes to God's call, and he equipped me for it, beginning my new walk with him. Don't get me wrong: I have been tempted to return to my treadmill ministry, and sometimes I do. It is safe—I can set the speed, the degree of difficulty, and the schedule of how often I do it. I can run on that spiritual treadmill for days, even weeks and months, until eventually I recognize how empty my soul is.

Take a moment and consider the week before you. What does your schedule look like? How will God be glorified and the Kingdom affected by your plans? Is your week full of good things or God things? Do you need to step off the treadmill in order to walk with God? Here are some things to think about:

What usually motivates you to accept a ministry opportunity?

In what ways might the devil be tempting you to serve God for the wrong reasons?

❧ POINT TO PONDER

Will you make it your goal to seek God's call and God's approval before you schedule your next time commitment? Warning: Don't say yes unless you mean it.

I have always enjoyed this little poem because there is great truth in its simplicity.

Mary had a little lamb;
It would have been a sheep.
It joined the local megachurch
And died from lack of sleep.

When Jesus was in the wilderness, he could have turned those stones to bread but he didn't. He could have acquired all the power and glory this world offered, but he didn't want it. He could have jumped from the Temple to prove he was God's Son, but he chose to remain in the desert. Jesus didn't come to this earth to show everyone his power and glory. He came to show God's. He didn't come to earth to live with wealth and power. He came to walk humbly to a cross. Jesus wasn't born to be just a great man or teacher. He was born to be the Messiah, and he is the living example for us to follow in our own ministries.

God was speaking to his exiled people in Jeremiah 29:11 when he said, *"I know the plans I have for you. . . . plans to prosper you and not to harm you, plans to give you hope and a future,"* (NIV). The key to that verse is found in the first sentence. Are you living God's plan or are you tempted to live your own? The health of your soul—and your eternal reward—depends on your answer. Don't be content to lead a good life designed to impress others. That temporary contentment is offered by the devil himself. Choose instead to fulfill God's plan for you. He calls you to be godly and rewards you eternally. Why settle for less!

Father, forgive us for the times we lead lives that give you no control and no glory. We confess that it is easier to think of you as Savior than Lord. Help us, God, to be filled with your Spirit so that when he reveals your call we are ready and anxious to serve. And may our hearts rejoice with praise for who you are. Amen.

DO YOU RECOGNIZE
THE VOICE OF GOD?

The morning was beautiful, the pews had been full, and my husband, Jim's, message had been well received. Sunday school was just beginning. I entered the classroom, attempting to give my best impression of what I thought a pastor's wife should personify. I was blissfully naive in those days and had so much to learn. I didn't want anyone to know just how unequipped and fearful I was of the title "pastor's wife," so I worked hard to *look* the part.

As our guest speaker moved gracefully toward the podium, I couldn't help noticing her feathered, teased, and heavily sprayed hair. West Texas women in the 1980s were known for having "big hair." But that wasn't all. She sported bright blue eye makeup and hot pink lipstick. When she walked past, she left behind a lingering trail of floral-scented perfume. Her dress was adorned with huge bows (the kind that made it almost impossible to sit straight in the pews) and puffy sleeves with shoulder pads so thick the entire soprano section of the choir would have been hidden from anyone who sat in the pew behind her.

The director of the Sunday school department told us that we were in for a *treat* that morning, which really meant, "Here is your substitute for the day because the regular teacher is skiing in Colorado." I took one look at the hot pink lipstick and patent leather shoes and felt quite certain that there was going to be no treat involved in this morning's lesson. In fact, I believed the only lesson I would learn that day would be a lesson in tolerance. But I quickly donned my best "preacher's wife smile" and sat prepared to give the appropriate spiritualized nods of encouragement and approval.

The guest speaker introduced herself and said her topic for that morning was her spiritual passion—prayer. I had heard that she had a reputation for being a *prayer warrior* (a person who prays often and powerfully). Our fabulously floral-scented fill-in teacher did a good job telling us about the importance of prayer. I think I nodded at least four or five times and might even have said "amen" a time or two.

I was fully in her corner until she said, "The most signifi-cant part of my prayer time comes toward the end, when I sit and listen for God's answers and wait for him to speak." (I decided to withhold my nod and amen momentarily.) She began to talk about how, by listening for God to speak, she had come to *recognize* the voice of God. "He speaks to my heart, offering me guidance and answers," she said con-fidently. I glanced nervously at the Sunday school director, hoping to read her mind. *I* was fairly certain our speaker was headed for left field. But the director was obviously enjoying the lesson, approving everything that our substitute was saying. Had the director heard what this woman had said? How could someone recognize God's voice and know when he spoke to her? I knew the director was a godly woman with great spiritual maturity, so I decided to keep listening. Besides, I didn't want to look like I was clueless about the spiritual aspects of prayer, even though I was.

At the end of the lesson I still had my doubts, but I was also extremely curious about her "truths." As it turned out, that lesson really was a treat. God, in his grace and patience with my youth, ignored my judgmental attitude and chose to bless me through that wonderful Christian woman . . . with her big Texas hair and her God-given wisdom. As I think about that Sunday morning, I realize how close I came to missing one of the most important lessons of my Christian life: Don't focus more on the messenger than the message. By the end of her thought-provoking lesson, I was determined to begin to listen and to understand that God *does* speak and we absolutely *can* recognize his voice.

RECOGNIZE THAT GOD'S VOICE WILL HELP AND COMFORT
Consider these verses:

O people of Zion, who live in Jerusalem, you will weep no more. He will be gracious if you ask for help. He will surely respond to the sound of your cries. Though the Lord gave you adversity for food and suffering for drink, he will still be with you to teach you. You will see your teacher with your own eyes.

Your own ears will hear him. Right behind you a voice will say, "This is the way you should go," whether to the right or to the left.   **Isaiah 30:19-21**

Isaiah was speaking to the nation of Israel, specifically to those who had wandered from God's teaching and were worshiping idols. Not only were their lives lacking the blessing of God, they were living with the consequences of their sin. They needed God's hope and his direction. The prophet Isaiah was sent to give both.

What encouragement was Isaiah able to promise the people of Zion?

What did their own ears hear and what did the voice behind them say?

Isaiah told the people of Zion that they had a gracious God who would listen. The only thing they needed to do was ask for help. They had disobeyed God and expected to be punished for their sin. Could this expectation have kept them from feeling like they could ask for divine help?

How many people never enter the door of a church because they think they aren't "good enough" to attend? Have you ever avoided prayer simply because you didn't believe you earned the right to ask God for anything? Isaiah told the Israelites that God would still be with them, to teach them, regardless of their past sins. How would he teach them? Their "own ears" would hear a voice that would direct them to the right path. If they would just ask, they would receive direction.

🕮 POINT TO PONDER

Do you ever expect to hear God's voice in your own ears to direct you?

REALIZE THAT GOD'S VOICE IS GOD'S WORD

Jesus taught his disciples how they could hear and know the voice of God. He told them:

There is so much more I want to tell you, but you can't bear it now. When the Spirit of truth comes, he will guide you into all truth. He will not speak on his own but will tell you what he has heard. He will tell you about the future. He will bring me glory by telling you whatever he receives from me. All that belongs to the Father is mine; this is why I said, "The Spirit will tell you whatever he receives from me." **John 16:12-15**

Who is the voice of God in our lives today?

Describe the things the Holy Spirit will reveal.

Who is glorified when the Holy Spirit speaks?

There have been thousands of sermons preached on the power of God in our lives through the Holy Spirit. We are taught that he is the source of our spiritual strength, our teacher, and our guide. He will always tell us the truth, and he will only speak what God has told him to say. For most of us, the problem is not in understanding or believing what God can do through the Spirit. The problem is in expecting it. During your week, do you schedule specific times in your days that offer an opportunity for the Holy Spirit to speak to you? Are there moments of your day when you find yourself more eager to listen? Do you expect God to speak during those times, or are you usually surprised when he does?

POINTS TO PONDER

Scripture reveals a great deal about the voice of God in our lives. Will you pray for the ability to discern God's voice and direction for your life as you listen to sermons, Bible lessons, advice, and your own prayer thoughts?

Trust That God's Voice Is True

God spoke and the world was created. He walked with Adam and Eve in the garden, conversing with them. God told Abraham to pack up and go until God told him to stop.

Moses heard God speaking from a burning bush (and even then had the audacity to argue!). In a vision Isaiah saw and heard God. Elijah heard God's still, small voice.

There are hundreds of examples of God speaking in the Old Testament. God spoke to the prophets and they, in turn, told the people what God wanted them to know. How could the prophets be certain it was God? Did they have a unique ability because they were "called"?

Jesus spoke to people and they listened. Wouldn't it have been an amazing privilege to be Mary and sit at Jesus' feet while he spoke? No wonder Jesus disciplined Martha for fussing in the kitchen. Paul had such a clear vision of Jesus that he changed his plan to turn east and went west to Macedonia instead. The apostle John was imprisoned on the island of Patmos when the Lord appeared and spoke to him. There Jesus instructed John to write down everything he said. We call it the Revelation. Everything God says is truth. How can we hear his truth today?

All Scripture is inspired by God. **2 Timothy 3:16**

Heaven and earth will disappear, but my words will never disappear. **Matthew 24:35**

When the Spirit of truth comes, he will guide you into all truth. He will not speak on his own but will tell you what he has heard. He will tell you about the future. **John 16:13**

God still speaks to his servants. The Word of God is exactly that. Do you just read Scripture or have you learned to *listen* to it? The moment you asked Jesus to be your Lord,

God saved you and you were given his presence, his power, and his *voice*! Have you taken time to know the One who longs to speak to you?

LISTEN SO THAT GOD'S VOICE BECOMES FAMILIAR

I am not a huge fan of cell phones. They go off at all the wrong times—in church, at conferences, and in restaurants. I especially hate it when they go off in the car. I like the bumper sticker that says, "Hang up the phone and drive!" My husband is always amazed when I actually answer my cell phone. I give very few people my mobile number because I don't want to be available all the time. Each day I like to have guaranteed quiet time.

However, if my cell phone rings at six thirty in the morning, I always jump for it as quickly as I can. I don't have to check the caller ID or guess who is calling so early; I know it's my mom. I don't need Mom to say anything more than hi because I know Mom's voice. I know if she is calling just to say hi or if she has something else on her mind, because I can hear it in her voice.

How is this possible? I know my mom, I love my mom, and I am interested in what she is going to say. I will always jump for her phone call because her calls always matter. Listening to God is a lot like listening for those phone calls from Mom. Do you love God and are you interested in what he has to say? Are you eager to hear him speak and sensitive to the times he is most likely to "call"?

Jesus was speaking to a crowd that consisted of his disciples, curious bystanders, and the church leaders who wanted to destroy him when he said,

"I tell you the truth, anyone who sneaks over the wall of a sheepfold, rather than going through the gate, must surely be a thief and a robber! But the one who enters through the gate is the shepherd of the sheep. The gatekeeper opens the gate for him, and the sheep recognize his voice and come to him. He calls his own sheep by name and leads them out. After he has gathered his own flock, he walks ahead of them, and they follow him because they know his voice. They won't follow a stranger; they will run from him because they don't know his voice." Those who heard Jesus use this illustration didn't understand what he meant, so he explained it to them: "I tell you the truth, I am the gate for the sheep. All who came before me were thieves and robbers. But the true sheep did not listen to them. Yes, I am the gate. Those who come in through me will be saved. They will come and go freely and will find good pastures. The thief's purpose is to steal and kill and destroy. My purpose is to give them a rich and satisfying life." **John 10:1-10**

I'm not surprised that the crowd didn't understand Jesus' illustration. Sheep are animals of low intelligence, and when left alone they are defenseless. People don't want to be compared to sheep. But when it comes to entering heaven, we are lost, defenseless sheep, in need of a Shepherd.

From the passage above, how are the sheep able to find the Shepherd and follow him to safety?

If you are saved, it is because you heard the voice of God and accepted his Son. You have entered the fold and you now have a Shepherd. Why is it important for us to listen for his voice?

Describe the lives of the sheep that follow their Shepherd.

☙ POINT TO PONDER

Does your life indicate that you have been listening for—and following—the voice of God?

To Jesus, we are sheep. In fact, he was being generous when he described us in that way. The Son of God could have said "housefly" or "slug" and still have been accurate. We like to think that we can plan our lives and schedules to make our own way through this world. The truth is that we are in continual need of God's never-ending care. We must know his voice in order to follow it. If we listen, we are safe. He promises us protection for our lives today and in the future. God loves you and calls you to him. How wonderful to imagine hearing our name called by the God who spoke the world into existence! How wonderful to know that his voice can be familiar, even to us sheep!

DISCERN GOD'S VOICE FROM ALL OTHERS

In today's world, the Shepherd's voice is definitely not the only voice that we hear. Jesus called the false teachers of his day thieves and robbers. Their message was intended to steal people away from discovering the truth. False teachers have always been shouting—and they always will. We live in a noise-filled world where Satan is allowed to speak to us and confuse us. But the sheep (that's us) have a Shepherd, and if we are listening for him, we can follow his voice. How do we learn to detect his voice from all the others? We pay attention to the moments when God is most likely to speak and the moments we are most likely to listen.

There are certain times when I tend to be open to "God thoughts." Most often, for a reason only God knows, he likes to speak to me at three o'clock in the morning. If I wake up during the night and the first number on the digital clock is three, I have learned to just say, "Yes, Lord?"

God brings to mind people I need to pray for or call that day. I confess things that I have said or done that I know have not pleased God, and I ask his forgiveness. Sometimes I need to do the same for people I have wronged in some way. I think of ideas or plans that constitute direction or the call of God. Sometimes God brings to my mind the Scripture passages he wants me to teach in my Bible study, and with his direction, the lesson begins to unfold in my mind. I have rewritten a lot of lessons during the wee hours of the morning.

At night, my mind isn't only filled with God thoughts; worries and fears seem to invade it too. There often seems to be a raging war in my head during those dark hours— with God on one side offering me instruction, mercy, or grace, and Satan on the other tormenting me with selfish desires, doubt, or fear. Perhaps God allows this battle because he knows in those hours of the night he is all I have to rely on. He reminds me of Scriptures that comfort me and provide strength or direction. God's answers enable me to lay those concerns at his feet and leave them there. I pay close attention to my thoughts during the predawn hours because so often they are the voice of God meeting my needs.

God speaks at other times as well. When my kids were young, I had to vacuum almost daily. Life was chaotic and noisy back then. If God wanted to speak to me, he would often wait until the vacuum would drown out all the other noises that came with a house full of kids. Often during the monotony of cleaning, I would hear the quiet "God thoughts." Now, as my house has become less hectic since the kids have left home, God sometimes speaks to me when I am driving in the car or just sitting with my coffee in the peaceful moments of the morning, before the noise of the day rushes in.

There are times when the words on the pages of my Bible seem to be highlighted with neon ink. I have sometimes missed the rest of a sermon or Bible study lesson because something was said that I know God intended for me to hear and think about. I have also discovered that God likes to talk to me when I am exercising. I am a walker, and more often than not, I find myself walking with my Savior, listening to his purpose for my day.

❧ POINTS TO PONDER

Can you describe the times when God is most likely to speak to you? What are you usually doing? Do you expect that God will speak to you at those times?

ALLOW GOD'S VOICE TO INTERRUPT YOUR SCHEDULE

Consider a passage from 1 Samuel 3. Hannah had presented her baby boy to Eli at the Tabernacle, fulfilling her promise to the Lord. Eli raised Samuel and taught him the Scriptures and the ways of God. One night, while Samuel was sleeping, he heard a voice call his name. Samuel assumed it was Eli calling and went to him three different times. The third time Samuel woke him, "Eli realized it was the LORD who was calling the boy" (verse 8).

> *So he said to Samuel, "Go and lie down again, and if someone calls again, say, 'Speak, LORD, your servant is listening.'" So Samuel went back to bed. And the LORD came and called as before, "Samuel! Samuel!" And Samuel replied, "Speak, your servant is listening."* **1 Samuel 3:9-10**

Eli was a prophet chosen by God to listen and then speak his message to the people. He taught Samuel how to respond to the voice of God. Allow him to be your teacher as well. He told Samuel to say:

"Speak, Lord"

Do you allow God to speak when he chooses?

"for your servant"

33

Are you a servant, ready to obey whatever word God gives you?

"is listening"

Do you live a life that is tuned to God's frequency, or is it difficult to hear him over the static?

Samuel would have been ready to listen if God had called to him on a Sabbath or as he was going about his daily tasks in the Tabernacle. There are times when we expect God to give us his word and direction, and he often does. But there are times when God calls with a message that is for the moment, at a time he has determined. Do you recognize God's voice well enough that he can speak when you are not expecting him to? I was sitting in church one Sunday morning when I noticed an attractive woman sitting by herself, crying. I had never seen her before, and I found myself praying for her. When the service ended I felt compelled to meet her. I introduced myself and invited her to Sunday school, where she was warmly received. A few weeks later she raised her hand and asked for prayer because she was on her way to Mayo Clinic for surgery. She had a rare disease that was considered fatal. The ladies in our class promised to pray for her, and they did—faithfully. The doctors at Mayo have no explanation for the woman's continued health, but the members of our class do. Our friend is God's miracle, and we are careful to give him the glory. What a privilege to be available to the Spirit when he speaks!

Are you willing to postpone your own schedule in order to fulfill God's? Servants don't tell their master they will "get around to it" or say, "I'm not quite able to do that today." Instead the servant says, "Speak at any time. You are Lord and I am not. I am ready to do anything you ask. You are the master and I will always be listening for your voice." God didn't ask us to be servants because he needs our help— he asked us to be servants so we would remember that we need his.

I wish I could say that the lessons of this chapter can be learned quickly and easily. For me, neither has been true. The world is an interesting place and difficult to "tune out." But I have found that the lesson Eli taught Samuel is still relevant for us today. I can sense when God is speaking to me and say, "Speak, Lord, for your servant is listening." I can now stand with the wonderful lady who taught me in her hot pink heels and say, "God has a voice and you can recognize him when he speaks." The question is never whether or not he wants to speak, but whether or not I choose to listen. I like this quote from Frederick Faber:

> There is hardly ever a complete silence in our soul. God is whispering to us well nigh incessantly. Whenever the sounds of the world die out in the soul, or sink low, then we hear these whisperings of God. He is always whispering to us, only we do not always hear because of the noise, hurry, and distraction which life causes as it rushes on.[2]

Heavenly Father, speak to me. I am your servant and I want to listen. Forgive me for the many times I have followed other voices and lost the sound of yours. Thank you for shouting sometimes when I wouldn't listen to your whisper. I love you and I know that all you say matters. Speak, Lord, for your servant is listening.

Three

RUNNING ON EMPTY?
RETREAT

I remember getting ready for my first silent prayer retreat. My sons, Ryan and Craig, were upstairs watching TV instead of getting ready for their baseball game. The phone was ringing because my husband needed to tell me he was running late. I had spent the day frantically doing laundry, grocery shopping, paying bills, and arranging for someone else to take the boys to school, a birthday party, and another baseball game. I still needed to prepare a Sunday school lesson and pack for a retreat I had *somehow* allowed myself to get talked into. My suitcase sat open on the bed, waiting to be packed. *What do you wear at a silent prayer retreat?*

I took a quick break to write my husband a note because the baseball uniforms would need to be washed that evening so they would be clean for the game tomorrow. Then I wrote a second note to remind Jim that if he washed the shirts in the same load as the pants, our boys would be wearing pink uniforms to the game. Even as I was writing the note, I knew that either those pants would stay dirty or be transformed to a rose-tinted hue, or the boys would be playing tomorrow's game in damp uniforms laundered thirty minutes before game time.

I glanced at the clock and yelled to the boys that if they didn't have those baseball uniforms on in the next two minutes they could just skip their games! Since they know that Mom rarely makes idle threats, I heard them turn off the television and *run* for their room.

My husband dashed in, apologizing that he was late and asking in the same breath, "Remind me again. Where do the boys need to be?" He glanced at my open suitcase and grinned. "You are going to *love* this retreat. I'm so glad you are getting some *time off.*" About that time one of the boys yelled down the stairs that he couldn't find his baseball cleats *anywhere*!

There are a lot of expressions that define moments like this: "that's the final straw"; "you just got on my *last* nerve"; "watch out, she's going to blow"—any expression would have been appropriate. I wish I would have taken a deep breath, said a little prayer, and responded in a soft, June Cleaver–like voice with positive words of encouragement and direction. Instead I heard someone sounding like Joan Rivers on a really bad day shout, "I do not have time for this retreat. Maybe other people can go sit on a bench for three days and pray . . . but that just isn't me. I have a life and I am too busy for this!" If we had had a dog, it would have run under a table.

In the end, my son found his cleats, my husband found out how to get to the ballpark, and my entire family hugged me and left me alone as quickly as they could. *Great!* I thought to myself. *If I die in a car accident on the way to this thing, that will be the last memory Jim has of his wife and the boys have of their mother. Nice job, Janet!*

I finished packing and drove to the monastery to join the rest of the group. My friend who had talked me into this retreat met me with a hug and a smile. "I'm so glad you are here," she said. I smiled back and said in my best pastor's wife tone, "Me too. I'm sure it will be a *wonderful* and *blessed* weekend with the Lord!" (I could always fake being spiritual when necessary.)

I found my room with its cinder block walls, twin bed, sink, and shower. There was no cable TV at the monastery. There wasn't even a clock or radio. I unpacked and decided to walk around the grounds until dinnertime. *The setting is beautiful,* I had to admit to myself. I took a deep breath and decided to give God a chance. *After all,* I thought, *I'm stuck at this place for the next three days, so I might as well make the most of it.*

Thus began my first silent prayer retreat. Our group ate dinner together on the first night, then the leader taught us about the value of silence and solitude from the Scriptures. When he finished speaking we were dismissed to spend the next forty-eight hours in complete silence. We saw each other at meals, smiling and waving at one another. At first the silence felt awkward, but slowly the quiet peace of God began to develop in my soul. God's presence was tangible, and his quiet voice was so clear. When we finally came together to break the silence, I was sorry it was over. I have tried to attend *every* silent prayer retreat offered since that time. I discovered my soul, and more important, I rediscovered my joy in Jesus during those few days. I have been blessed every time I have led or attended silent retreats since then.

Have you ever attended a retreat like that? Does the idea of meditation and contemplation sound like it belongs to an Eastern religion or is a New Age idea? Does solitude seem like something to avoid—or something to embrace?

I love Psalm 34:8, which says, "Taste and see that the LORD is good. Oh, the joys of those who take refuge in him!" A lot of things in this world are an acquired taste. No one in my family liked spinach the first time he tried it. My youngest son still won't eat cantaloupe. The first time I tasted coffee I thought it was terrible, but drinking it made me feel mature, so I just kept it up. Now one of my favorite things in this world is that first cup in the morning. I don't just want my coffee, I *need* my coffee.

Silence and solitude with God is a little bit like that. It might not sound very appealing at first, but if you experience silence, you will realize that you need it. Now that I have experienced extended time alone with God, I crave it more than I do my coffee. And trust me, that means it must be a huge craving! I believe silence and solitude are *essential* to a growing, maturing faith. Are you willing to "taste and see"?

GIVE YOUR SOUL A SABBATH REST

I always thought my soul was just the part of me that God saved, the part of me that would live eternally in heaven. I was a Christian a long time before I learned that the health of my soul was crucial to my spiritual life. Billy Graham said, "We take excellent care of our bodies which we have for only a lifetime; yet we let our souls shrivel which we will have for eternity."[3] Jesus prayed, "Give us this day our daily bread." I have always been taught that having daily time with the Lord is as important as eating each day. But as much as I enjoy it, it is not enough. Consider the fourth commandment:

Remember to observe the Sabbath day by keeping it holy. You have six days each week for your ordinary work, but the seventh day is a Sabbath day of rest dedicated to the LORD your God. On that day no one in your household may do any work. This includes you, your sons and daughters, your male and female servants, your livestock, and any foreigners living among you. For in six days the LORD made the heavens, the earth, the sea, and everything in them; but on the seventh day he rested. That is why the LORD blessed the Sabbath day and set it apart as holy.   **Exodus 20:8-11**

Why did God command us to have a Sabbath day?

Describe how a Sabbath day differs from every other day.

Now read what Jesus said about the Sabbath:

At about that time Jesus was walking through some grainfields on the Sabbath. His disciples were hungry, so they began breaking off some heads of grain and eating them. But some Pharisees saw them do it and protested, "Look, your disciples are breaking the law by harvesting grain on the Sabbath." Jesus said to them, "Haven't you read in the Scriptures what David did when he and his companions were hungry? He went into the house of God, and he and his companions broke the law by eating the sacred loaves of bread that only the priests are allowed to eat. And haven't you read in the law of Moses that the priests on duty in the Temple may work on the Sabbath? I tell you, there is one here who is even greater than the Temple! But you would not have condemned my innocent disciples if you knew the meaning of this Scripture: 'I want you to show mercy, not offer sacrifices.' For the Son of Man is Lord, even over the Sabbath!" **Matthew 12:1-8**

What examples did Jesus give the Pharisees to prove his disciples' innocence?

What Scripture did the Pharisees not understand? How are we tempted to be legalistic with the Sabbath today?

Look over both the Old Testament passage and the one from the New Testament. Does your soul experience a Sabbath rest each week?

I had never heard of blue laws until I moved to Houston, Texas. The blue law prohibited the sale of furniture, clothing, hardware, and appliances from Saturday evening until noon on Sunday. The law was an effort to enforce a degree of morality in the state and encourage church attendance.

We moved to Texas after my freshman year of college, and I was just getting involved in our family's new church. One Sunday as I was getting ready, I remembered that I needed a new pair of panty hose. I rushed to the grocery store, grabbed the familiar white plastic egg container, and quickly ran to the checkout counter. "You can't buy panty hose until 12:00 p.m. because of the blue law," the person at the register told me. After she explained what the blue law was, I said, "I need them for church—and church is *over* at 12:00 p.m." She wouldn't change her mind, so I drove to worship that morning with a run in one leg *and* a bad attitude.

Now I miss the blue law. The state of Texas used to say that Sunday mornings were for church attendance. Today Sunday isn't very different from Saturday, or any other day for that matter. What would happen in our world if, once again, the church started to observe and proclaim a Sabbath day? Would your family and friends complain about the inconvenience? Would your child's sports schedules be significantly altered? Imagine the local malls, empty on Sunday. What would all those people do if the stores were closed for the Sabbath?

I remember when the fast-food restaurant Chick-fil-A opened in the mall. They had to obtain special permission to stay closed on Sunday. Some people said the business would never survive without service on one of the busiest days of the week. But the restaurant founder, S. Truett Cathy, believed that God should be served on Sundays, not food. Of course, Chick-fil-A has been incredibly successful, even without being open on Sunday. Think of other businesses that would be blessed if they adopted a similar philosophy!

Picture a day, every week, filled with worship, ministry, and rest. Your family would probably be together because there would be no scheduled activities. Maybe you would get together with neighbors or friends because they would be home as well. Maybe you would take a long walk with your spouse or read a book to your child. Doesn't that sound like a *great* day? It isn't hard to imagine why God ordained a Sabbath day of rest.

We are commanded to have a day dedicated to the Lord, a day set apart for holy rest. Jesus said to use the day to offer God's love and mercy to others. God knew you needed a day each week to refuel your soul. What is happening to the souls of his children because the Sabbath is rarely observed? Scripture says, "Remember to observe the Sabbath day by keeping it holy." God knew what was necessary for his children to be spiritually healthy, which is why he made the Sabbath a commandment—not simply a suggestion.

❧ POINT TO PONDER

What would you need to change in order to have a Sabbath day of rest?

RETREAT FROM THE WORLD AND RENEW YOUR SOUL

I like theologian John Stott's "recipe" for a healthy soul, which my husband, Jim, has summarized as "An hour a day, a day a week, and a week a year."[4] Most Christians know they need to pray and study their Bibles each day. Most Christians understand that God created and set aside a day for rest. Both of those truths are taught in most churches. The vast majority of Christians *don't* understand how important and valuable it is to set aside an extended period of time for solitude and silence. We know about the hour a day, and the day a week, and to be honest, we struggle just to include those times in our schedules. How and why should we try to find time for a spiritual retreat?

It was the second year of Jesus' earthly ministry. Large crowds gathered everywhere he went. Matthew 14 describes a time in Jesus' life when he felt the need to retreat. He had recently been told that John the Baptist was dead, beheaded by Herod. Scripture says:

> *As soon as Jesus heard the news, he left in a boat to a remote area to be alone. But the crowds heard where he was headed and followed on foot from many towns. Jesus saw the huge crowd as he stepped from the boat, and he had compassion on them and healed their sick.* **Matthew 14:13-14**

The people were hungry and in a remote place, so Jesus performed a miracle by feeding the five thousand.

Immediately after this, Jesus insisted that his disciples get back into the boat and cross to the other side of the lake, while he sent the people home. After sending them home, he went up into the hills by himself to pray. Night fell while he was there alone.   **Matthew 14:22-23**

Why did Jesus seek solitude?

What are some of the words used in the verses above that indicate the urgency with which Jesus sought to be alone with God?

Jesus left the glory of heaven and came to live in our fallen world, choosing the limitations of a human body. He was at the height of his public ministry when he experienced the grief of losing someone he loved, his cousin John. Jesus continued to minister to all those around him until he realized that he needed to take some time to be alone with God. If Jesus needed to take time to renew his soul, so do you. When was the last time you were alone with God for the purpose of refilling your worn-out and weary soul? If you are waiting to *have* time, you may wait far too long.

There was never a time when Jesus wasn't aware of the

needs that surrounded him. He had crowds of people that were begging for his message and his miracles. Yet he walked away from even his disciples so that he could be alone with God. Jesus experienced moments of grief and exhaustion. During those times, he knew what was necessary. Do you?

POINT TO PONDER

Like Jesus, have you sought time alone with God?

BE STILL SO YOU CAN KNOW HE IS GOD . . . AND YOU AREN'T

Have you ever taken a time-management course? The phrase that defines efficiency is "multitasking." We admire people who can do several things at once, all with apparent ease. A person's life shouldn't consist of multiple tasks and the struggle to complete them. It should consist of divine opportunities and God's grace to accomplish them. Because once the assignments are done, God will give you the opportunity to rest.

The LORD is my shepherd; I have all that I need. He lets me rest in green meadows; he leads me beside peaceful streams. He renews my strength. He guides me along right paths, bringing honor to his name. **Psalm 23:1-3**

How did David benefit from his times of rest and quiet?

Be still, and know that I am God!   **Psalm 46:10**

Why does a Christian need to "be still"?

So often we believe that the person who manages to work more is somehow worth more. Instead, we should be impressed by the people who understand their need for God's rest and who speak from a quiet strength acquired from the peaceful streams of God. Look for the people who do what matters—the people who take time to "be still." They aren't trying to be a god; they are trying to know One.

✿ POINT TO PONDER

Scripture says, "Be still, and know that I am God!" Could it be that when we don't take time to be still and know God, other things become "gods" in our lives instead?

SEEK SILENCE

David and Moses spent hours alone while they tended flocks of sheep. Moses left the crowds and climbed to the top of Mount Sinai in order to speak to God. Jacob was alone when he wrestled with the angel. John the Baptist spent most of his life alone in the desert. Peter spent hours fishing. Imagine the hours and even days of silence that were a regular part of life during biblical times. The world seen in the Scriptures was very different from our world today. We rarely experience quiet moments unless we create them.

I grew up with three or four television stations that went off the air at night. My kids have a multitude of channels available twenty-four hours a day. We used to go to the theater for a movie, once or twice a month. How many movies on DVD do you own? I grew up with an AM radio. My kids can download thousands of songs into one MP3 player that they can carry in their pockets. We used to have one or two telephones that were hardwired to the wall of the house. Now it is difficult to finish a Sunday service or conference without hearing several cell phones ring.

We are *surrounded* by noise, making our need to retreat essential. We must be still to remember that *he is God.* Chuck Swindoll says, "I cannot be the man I should be without times of quietness. Stillness is an essential part of growing deeper."[5] Preacher Vance Havner says, "Jesus knows we must come apart and rest awhile, or else we may just plain come apart."[6] Paul was writing to the Christians in Thessalonica, instructing them how to live their earthly lives until Jesus returned, when he said:

> *Make it your goal to live a quiet life, minding your own business and working with your hands, just as we instructed you before. Then people who are not Christians will respect the way you live, and you will not need to depend on others.*
>
> **1 Thessalonians 4:11-12**

How does Paul describe a quiet life?

Do you think a quiet life would cause non-Christians to respect the way you live? Why?

When would the need to depend on others negatively reflect on your Christian witness?

There is very little about our world that is "quiet." Quiet lives don't impress other people. Quiet candidates are less likely to be elected. Quiet ministries don't have television programs. Quiet people rarely are chosen for the homecoming court. Paul would ask, "Would you rather impress people or God? Would you rather be popular or respected?"

Silence is not going to be something this world provides. If you don't intentionally seek silence, chances are you won't experience it. But silence is crucial for your soul and your life. There must be times in your life when the only sound you hear is the voice of God.

❧ POINT TO PONDER

What can you do to quiet your life and create necessary silence?

Jesus said,

Come to me, all of you who are weary and carry heavy burdens, and I will give you rest. Take my yoke upon you. Let me teach you, because I am humble and gentle at heart, and you will find rest for your souls. For my yoke is easy to bear, and the burden I give you is light.   **Matthew 11:28-30**

What should the purpose of a spiritual retreat be?

Jesus said, "Let me teach you." Why would a time of silence and solitude be an opportunity for that to happen?

❧ POINTS TO PONDER

When was the last time you retreated from the noise of this world to simply be alone with God? Is retreat a possibility, a probability, or a practice for you?

I came home from my first silent retreat with a very different attitude than the one I had brought to the retreat. I now plan regular times to turn the world off and spend quiet moments alone with the Lord. Those times may be for a few minutes in the morning or an entire day which I have intentionally scheduled for quiet. On Sunday mornings I try to shut off the program and work of church for the purpose of worship. At home, if there is work to be done on the Sabbath, it can usually wait until Monday. There are also times when I remain silent and contemplative for several days. When my soul is depleted and empty, I know the time has come for me to take God's hand and be led to the still waters where he will restore me. St. Clement of Rome prayed, "O God, make us children of quietness and heirs of peace."

Heavenly Father, I will quiet my life so you can awaken my soul. Help me ignore the momentary distractions for the sake of your eternal directions. I will be still . . . and know you are God.

Four

THE POWER OF PRIORITY

The family Bible sat on the coffee table in our living room for most of my childhood. I remember crawling up on the sofa and lifting the heavy book onto my lap so I could look at the pictures. The big white Bible had gold edges and was full of beautiful pictures depicting stories from Scripture. One picture especially fascinated me, and I always took the time to find it. The man in the illustration held a huge sword in one hand and a tiny baby, dangling by its foot, in his other hand. Two women knelt at the man's feet, one pleading with him while the other looked away. I couldn't comprehend how any man could be so evil, and I wondered what God would do about him. Perhaps that childhood memory prompted my lifelong fascination with King Solomon. I don't know when I learned that the man in the picture was actually proving his great wisdom. Solomon knew that the woman who was willing to give up her baby and spare its life was truly the baby's mother, rather than the imposter (1 Kings 3:16-28).

I've always been impressed with King Solomon's wisdom but have never understood some of his choices. He was the most successful, prosperous king in Scripture. Israel reached its highest level of power and prestige during his reign. And the nation would divide and fall, largely as a result of King Solomon's decisions.

Solomon wrote the book of Ecclesiastes at the end of his life, hoping to teach future generations and spare them his mistakes. He begins his book by saying, "Everything is meaningless . . . completely meaningless!" Not exactly the best way to grab a reader's attention and make her want to continue reading. That sentence would doom Ecclesiastes to the 75-percent-off table in the back of most Christian bookstores! Unfortunately, that one sentence has kept a lot of Christians from reading and concentrating on Solomon's book as well.

Ecclesiastes is Scripture, inspired and preserved by God. The author was a man who had experienced a long life, blessed by God's wisdom, a gift that he had asked God to give him. In this book, King Solomon wanted his readers to understand what really matters in life, as well as what will *not* matter after this life. Solomon taught that friendship is important: "Two are better than one, because they have a good return for their work: If one falls down, his friend can help him up. But pity the man who falls and has no one to help him up!" (Ecclesiastes 4:9-10, NIV). In Ecclesiastes 3:12 (NIV), he wrote about the value of being a kind person: "I know that there is nothing better for men than to be happy and do good while they live." (I would have preferred him to use the words "be godly" for the sake of this book.) Finally, Ecclesiastes 9:9 (NIV), a verse for your next anniversary card: "Enjoy life with your wife, whom you love, all the days of this meaningless life that God has given you under the sun—all your meaningless days. For this is your lot in life and in your toilsome labor under the sun." (An interesting verse from a man who had 700 wives and 300 concubines!) I think if Solomon could have lived his life again, he would have lived with a very different set of priorities. Ecclesiastes will probably not cheer you on a rainy day . . . in fact, you may need a long walk or some chocolate when you finish reading it. But if you approach the verses prayerfully, they can change your life.

Every day we are confronted with advertisements and advice about the best ways to spend our time and money. An advertising agency's job is to create ads that will persuade us that their product is worth considering—whether it is valuable enough to purchase now, later, or never. Whether it's written or not, we all have a personal list of priorities, some made sitting in a Sunday school class or Bible study and some revealed by our calendar appointments and checkbook registers. Hopefully, the lists are similar; for most of us, chances are they are significantly different. King Solomon would like to help reconcile those lists.

✄ POINTS TO PONDER

Who or what in your life has had the greatest influence on your value system? Where did you acquire your set of priorities?

Make Wisdom a Priority

Most candidates running for political office promise to improve the educational system in some way because they know it is important to the citizens they serve. Education and knowledge greatly benefit any nation, but they do not solve the moral problems that plague society if they are not used wisely. Charles Spurgeon said, "Wisdom is the right use of knowledge. To know is to be wise. . . . There is no fool so great as a knowing fool. But to know how to use knowledge is to have wisdom."[7]

POINTS TO PONDER

Is acquiring wisdom as important to you as earning an advanced degree? Do you recognize the difference between the two?

King Solomon, the son of David and Bathsheba, was a young man when he took the throne. God appeared to him in a dream and said, "What do you want? Ask, and I will give it to you!" (1 Kings 3:5).

Solomon replied, "You showed faithful love to your servant my father, David, because he was honest and true and faithful to you. And you have continued your faithful love to him today by giving him a son to sit on his throne. Now, O LORD my God, you have made me king instead of my father, David, but I am like a little child who doesn't know his way around. And here I am in the midst of your own chosen people, a nation so great and numerous they cannot be counted! Give me an understanding heart so that I can govern your people well and know the difference between right and wrong. For who by himself is able to govern this great people of yours?" **1 Kings 3:6-9**

Why did Solomon ask God for an understanding heart, for wisdom?

Under what circumstances are you most likely to seek God and ask for his wisdom?

What circumstances do you usually feel capable of handling on your own?

Someone once said, "Leaders are ordinary people with extraordinary determination." Solomon knew that to lead God's chosen people he would need to have wisdom greater than his own. So with "extraordinary determination" God's wisdom was exactly what he asked for.

Walk into any bookstore today and peruse the self-help literature. People seem to want to know about everything: career advancement or career change, medical diagnosis and treatment, how to catch a man or even how to unload one. You might see a book about finding deeper meaning in life right next to a book encouraging you not to take life so seriously. The topics covered seem endless. Sadly, Bibles are not found in the self-help section of the bookstores but rather sit alongside the Koran and New Age literature in the religion section of the store.

It's evident that people want help understanding themselves and their lives. Yet they seek only to be informed instead of becoming wise. It's like sitting in your car that has stopped running. *Ahh,* you think, *I'll just reach for that novel I've been reading about race cars and find the information I need,* while the owner's manual is sitting in the glove compartment. Our world today is looking in the wrong place for "self-help." The "owner's manual" is in a different section of the store.

❧ POINTS TO PONDER

When was the last time you sought God through prayer and Scripture, knowing that he alone had the perfect answer for your need? When was the last time you went to him first? When you are broken and in need of repair do you reach for the owner's manual or something else?

Enjoy the Blessing of Proper Priorities

Solomon asked God for the blessing of wisdom, for the sake of his people. So often our personal priorities are just that—personal. Jesus comes back to this same message in the New Testament when he taught his disciples not to worry about their individual needs. He said Solomon in all his glory was not dressed as beautifully as the lilies of the field (Matthew 6:25-32). Then Jesus told his disciples, "Seek the Kingdom of God above all else, and live righteously, and he will give you everything you need" (Matthew 6:33). Compare what Jesus said to his disciples with what God said to Solomon:

The Lord was pleased that Solomon had asked for wisdom. So God replied, "Because you have asked for wisdom in governing my people with justice and have not asked for a long life or wealth or the death of your enemies—I will give you what you asked for! I will give you a wise and understanding heart such as no one else has had or ever will have! And I will also give you what you did not ask for—riches and fame! No other king in all the world will be compared to you for the rest of your life! And if you follow me and obey my decrees and my commands as your father, David, did, I will give you a long life." **1 Kings 3:10-14**

What did Jesus say should be the highest priority for his disciples?

How does Solomon's request for wisdom illustrate the point Jesus was making?

In addition to riches and fame, what did God give Solomon?

What priorities did God require of Solomon?

Christians are taught to have two priorities: We are to follow the Word of God and obey the will of God. Those priorities keep us from having to worry about the cares of life. In fact, those priorities are the road to blessing. The difficulty is found, not in knowing the priorities of God, but in putting our own concerns in the same order. "Seek first" is God's instruction, but actually doing it is another matter.

Life is always going to present difficult decisions. When faced with hard choices my husband and I often find ourselves listing the pros and cons, thinking we can reach the right answer based on that list. In the end, we make our decision after we realize that our personal priorities may actually cloud our resolution rather than confirm it. There is only one "pro": the will of God. There is only one "con": refusing to obey it. How will we know what to do? We need to seek the wisdom of the King. Then we have nothing to worry about, except how to appreciate the blessing that follows.

❧ POINT TO PONDER

Do your priorities invite the blessing of God?

KNOW GOD AND YOU WILL KNOW WHAT MATTERS

Studying Solomon's life shows the abundant power and prosperity that the nation Israel achieved under his rule. God did give him riches and fame. Solomon built the Temple in Jerusalem, his breathtaking palace, and a large number of impressive community buildings. He brought advanced culture and education to the people of his day, and Jerusalem was esteemed throughout the world. He made trades and treaties with neighboring countries, often through marriage agreements. Israel lived in relative peace during this time but often compromised its own culture and belief system as a price for that peace. King Solomon gained more wealth, fame, and power than any other king in biblical history. But at the end of his life he wrote the words found at the end of Ecclesiastes. These were Solomon's final words of wisdom:

That's the whole story. Here now is my final conclusion: Fear God and obey his commands, for this is everyone's duty. God will judge us for everything we do, including every secret thing, whether good or bad. **Ecclesiastes 12:13-14**

What does Solomon say is the conclusion of all he has learned in life?

Why is that conclusion applicable to our lives too?

PURSUE THE POWERFUL PRIORITIES OF THE POWERFUL GOD
To "fear God" is to live in reverent awe of who he is. Think of Isaiah, seeing God in the Temple, "high and exalted" (Isaiah 6:1, NIV). Verse 5 describes Isaiah, overcome with his own unworthiness, and humble in the presence of God. Jesus taught us to pray, "Our Father in heaven, may your

name be kept holy" (Matthew 6:9). The current trend in churches today is to teach and preach about an approachable God. He is a God of grace and love, forgiveness and mercy. He is also the Creator God. And he is the God who judges. He is the God who is perfect, holy, and knows all things. God is, and always has been, approachable. Solomon, however, teaches that we should approach God thoughtfully, with the reverent awe that comes from knowing and respecting *all* that he is.

When I was a college student, I taught a children's Bible class. I wasn't exactly sure what I should do with a room full of noisy three- and four-year-olds. But they seemed to enjoy listening to the Creation story and hearing about the God who made everything. When the story was finished, I gave them paper and crayons and asked them to imagine what God looked like and draw him.

The room was quiet for a while as they drew. When everyone finished, I had them show their pictures to the class. Of course, there were drawings of men in long robes and white beards. There were also pictures of sunshine and bunnies. But one boy's picture intrigued me the most. He had drawn a man wearing a blue and gray shirt with a big number twelve on it. "Could you tell us about your picture?" I asked him. "I think God is like Roger Staubach" (the famous Dallas Cowboys quarterback at the time), he said, much to my surprise. "When Roger Staubach tells the team what to do, they *do it*!" he said enthusiastically. Excellent theology—from a four-year-old. Solomon said, "Fear God and obey his commands, for this is everyone's duty."

✵ POINT TO PONDER

Do you think of God and approach him in prayer with the "fear" that Solomon describes?

THINK OFTEN ABOUT YOUR PRIORITIES

There's no arguing that we live in the "age of information." The news channels report world events twenty-four hours a day. The Internet supplies answers to our questions as fast as we can type them. I remember spending hours in the library researching a term paper. Now my sons can write their papers and turn them in without ever leaving their rooms. Will the accessibility of information replace the need for knowledge? Will we make an effort to remember what we can ask again so easily? My dad worked for IBM. Their corporate slogan centered on one word—Think. The computer I use is proof that they did.

Solomon teaches us to make wisdom and the fear of God priorities in our lives. Wisdom and respect for God give us the strength needed to obey his commands. How do we acquire wisdom? We have to think. Solomon writes, in Proverbs chapter 2:

My child, listen to what I say, and treasure my commands.
Tune your ears to wisdom, and concentrate on understanding.
Cry out for insight, and ask for understanding.
Search for them as you would for silver; seek them like hidden treasures.

Then you will understand what it means to fear the LORD, *and you will gain knowledge of God.*

For the LORD *grants wisdom! From his mouth come knowledge and understanding.*

He grants a treasure of common sense to the honest. He is a shield to those who walk with integrity.

He guards the paths of the just and protects those who are faithful to him.

Then you will understand what is right, just, and fair, and you will find the right way to go.

For wisdom will enter your heart, and knowledge will fill you with joy.

Wise choices will watch over you. Understanding will keep you safe.   **Verses 1-11**

How does a person learn to fear God and know who he is?

What is the benefit to your life when you gain wisdom and understanding?

All of us should desire the wisdom to know God and understand his ways. There is no information available that's more valuable. How much money do we spend chasing illusions of gods who aren't real? Even Christians oftentimes place higher value on the wisdom of men than on the Word of God. We are quick to call a friend or tune in to a talk show that addresses our concerns. We rush to buy the latest best sellers from the local bookstore. The Lord grants wisdom. Are you expecting to find it anywhere else?

POINTS TO PONDER

What does "fearing God" mean to you? What means do you take to understand who he is?

INVEST IN GOD'S PRIORITIES

Today's society makes it difficult to live as Solomon suggested. Human nature defines "enough" as just a little bit more. We are bombarded by images that cause us to want what is new and think what we have is no longer valuable. The ads tell us if we haven't bought the latest and greatest then our clothes are outdated and our computers are too slow. Does your cell phone only allow you to make phone calls? Does your car have an onboard navigation system that gets you to your destination, or do you have to use a map? Does the "need for new" carry a high priority in your life? Maybe the problem is not that we want more. Maybe the weakness is found in *what* we want. Solomon writes:

Honor the LORD with your wealth and with the best part of everything you produce. Then he will fill your barns with grain, and your vats will overflow with good wine. My child, don't reject the LORD's discipline, and don't be upset when he corrects you. For the LORD corrects those he loves, just as a father corrects a child in whom he delights. Joyful is the person who finds wisdom, the one who gains understanding. For wisdom is more profitable than silver, and her wages are better than gold. Wisdom is more precious than rubies; nothing you desire can compare with her. She offers you long life in her right hand, and riches and honor in her left. She will guide you down delightful paths; all her ways are satisfying. Wisdom is a tree of life to those who embrace her; happy are those who hold her tightly. **Proverbs 3:9-18**

What should be our financial priority?

What should we want more than material possessions? Why?

I love "stuff" as much as the next person and more than some. My closet has too many clothes, too many shoes, and too many purses. I like nothing more than being at the department store when they open the doors and making my way to the 75-percent-off racks that display my favorite brands. I lead a workshop titled "The Coupon Queen of the Clearance Sale." I talk about using the money God has given to the fullest extent. My closest friends know that I am frugal. Actually they know I'm cheap—but frugal sounds kinder. They know that one of my favorite pastimes is to watch QVC every morning to see what "Today's Special Value" is for that day. The fact that I use coupons and shop clearance sales and the shopping channel doesn't necessarily mean I have more money. The truth is I just simply have more stuff. Spiritually, I don't have a problem giving my tithe. My problem may exist with what I do with the other 90 percent!

I need to be more excited about finding the wisdom of God than I am about finding my favorite brand on that clearance rack. I have enough stuff. But I will never have enough wisdom. God has made it clear what is most precious to seek and to find.

POINTS TO PONDER

Where do you look for treasures? Do you own life's most lucrative investments?

SUBMIT YOUR PRIORITIES TO GOD

King Solomon reached the end of his long and successful life and described it as "meaningless—like chasing the wind" (Ecclesiastes 1:14). The king had pursued the wealth, fame, power, and fulfillment the world provides. He acquired more than any human being ever had through hard work and strategy. But the book he wrote at the end of his life was about what he learned, not what he accomplished. Solomon said, "Here now is my final conclusion: Fear God and obey his commands, for this is everyone's duty."

Why is it our duty to love and respect God and live in obedience to his Word?

> *Because that is the path to joy.*
> *Because that is the life God can reward eternally.*
> *Because God loves us and wants the best for his children.*

Because the power of that priority will release the power of God in our lives.

How do we learn to live with God's priorities?

Pursue the wisdom of God.

The power of that one priority gives perspective to all others.

Get wisdom. Though it cost all you have, get understanding.
Proverbs 4:7, NIV

If you need wisdom, ask our generous God, and he will give it to you. **James 1:5**

Fear of the LORD is the foundation of true wisdom. All who obey his commandments will grow in wisdom. **Psalm 111:10**

Wisdom is yours for the asking. Do you make it a priority to ask often? You can search for help in many places. Have you made it a priority to search the Scriptures for the perfect answers from your perfect Father? New clothes, new sofas, new cars, and new stuff can give momentary happiness. Eternal joy comes from knowing you have found the most valuable commodities available to you. Wisdom and understanding are precious jewels, and they are your highest priority. May your heavenly crown reflect the fact that you understood the treasure gained from living by God's priorities.

🕮 POINT TO PONDER

Is the wisdom of God the priority of your life?

A PRAYER FOR WISDOM

Once again, Father, I have to confess
I ignored your abundance to choose something less.
Why did I blindly assume I was right?
You gave me your Word to be used as my light.

Free me, Lord, from the need to possess.
I ignored your abundance and gained something less.
It's your priorities that constitute need.
This life is a dance; I need you to lead.

Your wisdom, O God, is my promised success.
I will choose your abundance and ignore all things less.
Will you lead me to truth and teach me to think?
I promise to listen. I trust you to speak.

*Grant us your wisdom, O God. Remind us that everything
else is imperfect or potentially flawed. May this life be a
treasure hunt, a search for all that matters. You are the
foundation of wisdom. Help us to stand firm, refusing to
chase the wind. Amen.*

Five

IN THE DESERT,
BUT NOT DESERTED

My husband was called to his first full-time pastorate in 1984 when we were both twenty-five years old. Jim was still a seminary student, and I was teaching second grade. It was a small country church averaging about forty people on most Sundays. The church budget was limited, so a parsonage was provided as part of the pastor's salary. The house had been moved from a Dallas neighborhood to the back of the church parking lot and placed on a cinder block foundation. I spent a week cleaning and painting the house before we moved in. For five years, we called it home.

Jim and I were so excited to bring Ryan, our firstborn, home from the hospital to that parsonage. My maternity leave was for six weeks, but in order to fulfill my teaching contract I had to return to school for a month, so Jim cared for Ryan while I was teaching. It was the last time that I would work full-time out of the home. We had very little money, but I was able to stay home with Ryan and keep within our budget by shopping at garage sales for baby clothes and toys and by using grocery coupons from the Sunday paper. I had always wanted to be a mom and had looked forward to motherhood for the six years Jim and I had been married.

The fall came and went while I washed diapers and baby clothes and took care of Ryan. Jim pastored the church, was a full-time Ph.D. student, and taught an undergraduate class. Needless to say, he was very busy, and I was often lonely. The members of our church were wonderful to us. I still have the handmade crocheted blankets and teddy bears they gave to Ryan. I'd often find a gift of homegrown produce at the front door of the parsonage. I loved the church, but I found myself missing the house we had left, along with our community of friends. There were a few times when Ryan and I were home alone that a car pulled into the church parking lot and just parked. I didn't know why it was there; it made me nervous. I would hold Ryan and watch out the window, hoping whoever it was would drive away. They always did.

When my college friends, all married by this time, wrote or called, they would tell me about the new house they had just bought or the vacation they were planning to take. Meanwhile, Jim and I carefully managed each dollar, hoping neither of our cars would need major repairs.

One evening I sat watching Jim as he finished the dinner dishes for me. *I love him so much,* I thought. Almost immediately, another thought flashed through my mind. *But I'm not sure if I want to be a pastor's wife. Not if it means living at the edge of a parking lot and feeling lonely and scared.* I loved the people of the church, but I had no friends—no one my age, with a baby, who could just talk about first-time mom things. I knew rationally that these thoughts and worries couldn't be from God, but I couldn't stop myself emotionally from thinking them anyway. It was the first spiritual "desert" I ever remember experiencing. There I was, the preacher's wife, floundering, and there was no one to tell. I wish I had known then what I know today. Walking with God means allowing him to lead you to the desert once in a while.

Moses grew up in Pharaoh's royal family, received a good education, and was guaranteed a successful future. But Moses helped save an Israelite slave and found himself fleeing for his life. He went from the luxury of Pharaoh's palace to a tent in the desert. But there in that desert, Moses encountered the burning bush.

After Jacob had been given the bulk of his father's inheritance, he had to leave everything he had been given to escape his brother's certain wrath. Jacob had no way of knowing that he would meet Rebekah, his future wife, a short time later.

David spent day after day alone in the fields watching sheep. He had a lot of spare time and used it to hone his skills with his slingshot. Little did he know how much his extra practice would matter when he squared off with Goliath.

Joseph must have felt desperate as he sat in an Egyptian jail cell, accused of a crime he never committed. Truthfully, he was in jail *because* he had acted in a godly manner. It would have been difficult to trust the hand of God under those circumstances. Then one day Joseph, with God's help, interpreted a couple of dreams for Pharaoh, and the rest of Joseph's life fell into place. Scripture provides one example after another of God's children struggling to understand the trials they had to endure. Each of them would discover the purpose of their desert times, although for most of them that purpose was rarely clear at the time they were going through the hardship.

DESERTS ARE DESTINED

There are certain preachers who say that if you just live according to God's plan, you are guaranteed a life full of joy, happiness, peace, and health. Don't be fooled into thinking that "guarantee" is scriptural truth. Every committed Christian I know has hit a spiritual wall, or several of them, during his or her lifetime. Scripture does not promise an easy life, free from problems. In fact the Word of God promises exactly the opposite. Consider these words of Jesus:

> *But the time is coming—indeed it's here now—when you will be scattered, each one going his own way, leaving me alone. Yet I am not alone because the Father is with me. I have told you all this so that you may have peace in me. Here on earth you will have many trials and sorrows. But take heart, because I have overcome the world.*   **John 16:32-33**

Jesus was speaking to his disciples, trying to warn them about their future after his crucifixion. Jesus would face his most difficult days alone. What brought him encouragement during that time?

Why did Jesus warn his disciples that these things would happen to them, too?

What was the promise to the disciples then, and for us today, about life on earth?

Why should every disciple of Christ "take heart"?

Jesus spent almost every moment of his three-year ministry with his disciples, leading up to his death for them on the cross. Jesus knew the disciples would desert him during his most difficult days, but Jesus wasn't pitying himself or grieving for himself. Rather, Jesus warned the disciples, to protect them from the hardship *they* would face. Jesus promised them peace, but that wasn't his only promise. He encouraged them that after their earthly life, eternity would be easy; however, he also assured them that in this world, there would be struggles. Jesus told them with certainty that at times this world would be a difficult place for them, just as it had been difficult for him. Trials and sorrows were as much a promise for the disciples as the peace of God was to help them endure the trials.

God's promises abound in Scripture. When you are in the midst of difficult times, remember that desert times are a part of every disciple's life. My husband likes to say, "The holiness of God requires him to redeem all that he permits or causes." God has a plan for your life, a plan that includes time in the desert.

DESERTS ARE FOR DISCIPLINE

Some deserts are a consequence of our choices or the choices of those we care about. Proverbs 3:11-12 says, "My child, don't reject the LORD's discipline, and don't be upset when he corrects you. For the LORD corrects those he loves, just as a father corrects a child in whom he delights."

My children were raised in the time-out era. Most of the moms I knew had a chair where a child took a time-out in order to calm down and think about what he or she had done. We had a time-out chair, and most of the time it worked pretty well. God uses that same technique in our lives. Sometimes we need a "time-out," so God provides one. Saul (who would be known as Paul) was given the ultimate time-out on the road to Damascus.

Meanwhile, Saul was uttering threats with every breath and was eager to kill the Lord's followers. So he went to the high priest. He requested letters addressed to the synagogues in Damascus, asking for their cooperation in the arrest of any followers of the Way he found there. He wanted to bring them—both men and women—back to Jerusalem in chains. As he was approaching Damascus on this mission, a light from heaven suddenly shone down around him. He fell to the ground and heard a voice saying to him, "Saul! Saul! Why are you persecuting me?" "Who are you, lord?" Saul asked. And the voice replied, "I am Jesus, the one you are persecuting! Now get up and go into the city, and you will be told what you must do." The men with Saul stood speechless, for they heard the sound of someone's voice but saw no one! Saul picked himself up off the ground, but when he opened his eyes he was blind. So his companions led him by the hand to Damascus. He remained there blind for three days and did not eat or drink. **Acts 9:1-9**

What was Saul's mission in Damascus?

Why would Jesus say that Saul was persecuting him?

Describe how Jesus disciplined Saul.

Why do you think Jesus wanted Saul to experience what he did?

POINT TO PONDER

Why might God choose to discipline his children with "desert times"?

Spiritual deserts can be time-outs arranged by God. Just as all good parents want to correct wrong behavior in the children they love, God, our perfect Father, wants to discipline his children perfectly. We must consider the possibility that the difficult times of life may have been allowed or even caused by our loving Father. I know people who experienced financial crisis that led them to a deeper faith in God. One man confessed that he had not allowed God to be Lord of his business affairs, and he had in fact knowingly cheated others. The businessman fought bankruptcy, realizing that his circumstances were the direct discipline of the God who loved him.

I counseled a woman who had divorced and remarried. Her father had always been her spiritual role model, and then one day he shocked everyone by announcing that he was divorcing his wife and marrying his secretary. This one act influenced the daughter's choice to divorce her husband. When she became disenchanted with her own marriage, she felt that she had permission to end it because it was the option that her father had chosen. The woman I was counseling confessed between her tears that she had made a mistake divorcing her first husband, but knew she would need to stay married to her second husband. Because she had left her first husband so quickly, she hadn't considered all of her choices or all of the consequences. A desert time of discipline had brought her to a place of understanding. Together we prayed that God, in his perfect grace, would redeem her choices for his glory.

On occasion, I've heard Romans 8:28 quoted incompletely and incorrectly by well-meaning Christians to justify God bringing trials into our lives. Attempting to encourage another person, they say, "And we know that God causes everything to work together for the good . . ." I used to be one of those well-meaning Christians. Romans 8:28 is only truth when quoted in its entirety. "And we know that God causes everything to work together for the good of those who love God and are called according to his purpose for them." The Scripture promises that our mistakes can be redeemed and transformed for the good—but the promise is only for the person who loves God and wants to follow his will. Sometimes God leads us to a desert time until we remember the One we love most. In those solitary periods when he is our only source of refuge, we can begin to understand his calling for us and adjust our lives to that purpose.

Not all desert times are the result of our disobedient acts. Not all desert times are for the purpose of discipline. But if you find yourself in a desolate time and sense a separation from God, consider the possibility that he may have led you to the desert of discipline. Every Christian occasionally requires a time-out. Our perfect Father will discipline us for the sin in our life perfectly. It's part of his way to help us mature.

And I am certain that God, who began the good work within you, will continue his work until it is finally finished on the day when Christ Jesus returns. **Philippians 1:6**

DESERTS ARE FOR DIRECTION

When our children were younger and needed a time-out, I would set the kitchen timer for a designated number of minutes and send them to the time-out chair. Ryan and Craig were always ready to hop down and get back to their own agenda when the timer dinged, signaling that the disciplinary action was over. But most of the time they had to wait for "the talk." The time spent sitting still in the chair was the discipline. The talk was to make sure each boy had learned his lesson and knew how to behave in the future. The desert times of discipline are almost always followed by a time to talk with God and make sure we are "called according to his purpose." Often we are led to a desert time for the purpose of receiving new direction from God.

Are you content with your life and the good things you have accomplished? God may be calling you to a higher level of commitment in your Christian walk or ministry, a call you may not hear unless he leads you to a quiet desert, away from your comfortable circumstances. The deserts of direction are intended to isolate you from the world and present you with God's new plan. Whether you welcome the change or not, every Christian is asked to be willing to change, whenever God introduces the need. It was true for men and women in biblical times, too.

God told Moses to command Pharaoh to free the Israelites from slavery. Moses' response? The Hebrew equivalent of "You have to be kidding!" When David was anointed king of Israel, he had to endure twenty-five years of desert time before he took the throne. Mary rushed back to the Temple looking for her twelve-year-old son, and found him amazing the rabbis with his questions. When she asked Jesus why he had stayed behind, he told her, "I had to be about my Father's business." Scripture says she "stored" her thoughts in her heart (Luke 2:51). I imagine she had a lot to think about on the long walk home. Sometimes God calls us to step out and follow his direction in ways that will require increased strength and faith. Often these calls are given during or following time in the desert.

Imagine Ananias's face when the Lord spoke to him in a vision and said, "Go over to Straight Street, to the house of Judas. When you get there, ask for a man from Tarsus named

Saul. He is praying to me right now. I have shown him a vision of a man named Ananias coming in and laying hands on him so he can see again" (Acts 9:11-12). Ananias sounded like Moses when he answered, "But Lord . . . I've heard many people talk about the terrible things this man has done to the believers in Jerusalem! And he is authorized by the leading priests to arrest everyone who calls upon your name" (Acts 9:13-14). How often do you and I respond to God's call by pointing out to him why his plan can't possibly work! Thankfully God is just as patient with us as he was with Ananias.

The Lord said to Ananias, "Go, for Saul is my chosen instrument to take my message to the Gentiles and to kings, as well as to the people of Israel. And I will show him how much he must suffer for my name's sake" (Acts 9:15-16). Scripture says that Ananias obeyed God and went looking for Saul. When he found Saul, Ananias spoke to him, the scales fell from Saul's eyes, and he was baptized. Saul of Tarsus, or Paul as he became known, stayed in Damascus preaching about Jesus in the synagogues (Acts 9:17-20). It seemed like God's plan was complete.

But God had another plan for Paul's ministry, one that the Jewish convert would probably not been willing to accept. Paul would require a desert time of direction. Paul spent an unknown amount of time in Damascus after his conversion. When his preaching began to create significant problems for the Jewish leaders, some of them decided to kill Paul, so he escaped to Damascus and fled to the desert of Arabia.

Paul wrote about his desert time in the first chapter of

Galatians. He wanted the church in Galatia to understand his life and God's call for him. He wrote:

Dear brothers and sisters, I want you to understand that the gospel message I preach is not based on mere human reasoning. I received my message from no human source, and no one taught me. Instead, I received it by direct revelation from Jesus Christ. You know what I was like when I followed the Jewish religion—how I violently persecuted God's church. I did my best to destroy it. I was far ahead of my fellow Jews in my zeal for the traditions of my ancestors. But even before I was born, God chose me and called me by his marvelous grace. Then it pleased him to reveal his Son to me so that I would proclaim the Good News about Jesus to the Gentiles. When this happened, I did not rush out to consult with any human being. Nor did I go up to Jerusalem to consult with those who were apostles before I was. Instead, I went away into Arabia, and later I returned to the city of Damascus. Then three years later I went to Jerusalem to get to know Peter, and I stayed with him for fifteen days. The only other apostle I met at that time was James, the Lord's brother. I declare before God that what I am writing to you is not a lie. After that visit I went north into the provinces of Syria and Cilicia. And still the Christians in the churches in Judea didn't know me personally. All they knew was that people were saying, "The one who used to persecute us is now preaching the very faith he tried to destroy!" And they praised God because of me.   **Galatians 1:11-24**

Although theologians aren't certain whether or not Paul spent exactly three years in Arabia, most believe he was in the desert for a long period of time. Look at the passage above and describe the new direction the Holy Spirit wanted to reveal to Paul during his desert time.

What did Paul want the church to understand about the gospel message he preached? What did Paul want them to understand about the message giver?

What does Paul's experience teach us about our own desert times? Who does Paul recommend as our counselor when we go through those periods?

🎴 POINT TO PONDER

How will Paul's experience help you handle the next "desert time" in your own life?

Paul was not only a student of the famous teacher Gamaliel, but he was also a Pharisee of Pharisees. He describes himself as being "far ahead of [his] fellow Jews" in his zeal for the laws and traditions of his Jewish faith. His conversion experience shattered everything he had been taught throughout his life. Because the Messiah, Jesus Christ, had spoken to Paul, he would need to rethink everything; his entire life was about to be changed forever.

Even today, the Arabian desert is a desolate, barren place. Yet in this wasteland Paul sought the counsel of God. The

Holy Spirit chose that desert to lead Paul to the truths that he would teach and preach for the rest of his life. Paul was the apostle who would teach Christian doctrine to infant churches and lead Old Testament believers to become New Testament Christians. His days in the desert gave Paul the direction he needed to fulfill his call. Paul realized that by God's grace, he was to take the gospel to the Gentiles. His whole life had been preparing him for that call.

Moses couldn't imagine confronting Pharaoh and telling him to set God's people free. Ananias couldn't imagine ministering to the persecutor of Christians, Saul of Tarsus. Paul would have been equally confused by a call to preach to the Gentiles. Devout Jews despised Gentiles and made every effort to avoid them. However, when Paul was in the desert, he came to a new understanding, through the revelation of Christ, of God's direction and love for all people.

There are times when God wants to give you direction, and like Ananias, you will obey without hesitation. Other times you may not listen or you may hear but choose not to be obedient. At these times God simply needs to draw you away to the desert, where, alone with him, you can clearly hear him. You may also want to talk about your struggle with more mature Christians who have experienced trials in their spiritual walks. But first and foremost, seek God's perfect wisdom.

God wants you to listen to him. Remember Solomon's wise words the next time you find yourself in the desert waiting for direction. "Trust in the LORD with all your heart; do not depend on your own understanding. Seek his will in all you do, and he will show you which path to take" (Proverbs 3:5-6).

DESERTS OFFER DELIVERANCE

My sons have outgrown the time-out chair—we gave it away
years ago. The chairs we take time-outs in today are selected for
rest and comfort. We each have a favorite spot, and when we
relax there, we know we are home. Interestingly enough, God
designates desert time for comfort too. Isaiah 35 is a beautiful picture of comfort and hope that the prophet gave to the
Jewish nation. It spoke of the day when God would restore
them to their homeland and they would know his peace. God
calls his people to this desert so they can marvel at his ability to
restore their souls. I love the description in this chapter:

> *Even the wilderness and desert will be glad in those days.*
> *The wasteland will rejoice and blossom with spring crocuses. Yes,*
> *there will be an abundance of flowers and singing and joy! The*
> *deserts will become as green as the mountains of Lebanon, as*
> *lovely as Mount Carmel or the plain of Sharon. There the LORD*
> *will display his glory, the splendor of our God. With this news,*
> *strengthen those who have tired hands, and encourage those who*
> *have weak knees. Say to those with fearful hearts, "Be strong, and*
> *do not fear, for your God is coming to destroy your enemies. He*
> *is coming to save you." And when he comes, he will open the eyes*
> *of the blind and unplug the ears of the deaf. The lame will leap*
> *like a deer, and those who cannot speak will sing for joy! Springs*
> *will gush forth in the wilderness, and streams will water the*
> *wasteland. The parched ground will become a pool, and springs*
> *of water will satisfy the thirsty land. Marsh grass and reeds and*
> *rushes will flourish where desert jackals once lived. And a great*
> *road will go through that once deserted land. It will be named*
> *the Highway of Holiness. Evil-minded people will never travel*

on it. It will be only for those who walk in God's ways; fools will never walk there. Lions will not lurk along its course, nor any other ferocious beasts. There will be no other dangers. Only the redeemed will walk on it. Those who have been ransomed by the LORD will return. They will enter Jerusalem singing, crowned with everlasting joy. Sorrow and mourning will disappear, and they will be filled with joy and gladness. **Isaiah 35:1-10**

How will God's people be protected in the desert?

How will God provide for them in the desert?

How will God restore their passion for holiness in the desert?

What makes the desert an ideal place to know the power and deliverance of God?

🕮 POINT TO PONDER

Are you able to praise God for the desert times you have experienced in your lifetime?

It has been over twenty years since I sat in the kitchen of that country parsonage and questioned whether or not I was cut out to be a pastor's wife. God brought me to a desert so that he could reveal his plan for my future. Over time I learned to live in my humble surroundings, grateful for the home it provided my family. The material things I thought I needed were no substitute for the love my husband and I shared. And my definition of friends changed too. Friends don't have to be the same age or share the same interests. Friends are people who love you and treat you with kindness. I needed the perspective that the desert gives to remember that I had been blessed abundantly. Without it, I never would have changed or moved forward spiritually.

I have been back to the spiritual desert several times since, always wishing I could leave when I got there and always grateful that I stayed. I have learned to appreciate the desert for all it provides and teaches, even though my appreciation may not come except in retrospect.

When you find yourself in the desert, make a point to rely on the promises of God. So often when we fail to hear God's voice or our walks seem dry, we analyze his absence from an emotional level. We begin to doubt our self-worth (or our God-worth) and ultimately begin to doubt God's plans for our lives. Don't waste time relying on your own human reasoning; make every second count while you're in the wilderness and remember the principles taught in the Word of God.

- Know you are loved. God has led you to the desert or allowed you to go for a reason.
- Ask God if there is anything you need to confess. Is the desert a consequence of your choices and for your discipline?

- Remember that God often takes you to the desert so he can refocus or redirect your life. Is it possible that there is a change coming that God wants to prepare your heart and mind for?
- Be still and know that he is God. Embrace the loneliness because it is a time when you can seek the face and compassion of your Father.
- Seek the word of God before you seek the counsel of others. God brought you to the desert to listen to him. Don't be distracted from what he wants to say.
- God will decide when to bring you out of the desert. Don't be sidetracked by the world's diversions. These distractions can help you forget you are in the desert temporarily, but they cannot bring you out of it.
- Expect that the desert times will come. What will you do the next time you find yourself there?

It's tough in the desert. It's bewildering. It's destructive. It's hellish. Yet the testimony of the Old Testament, and ever more strongly, of the New, is that out of it comes new growth, new insight, new certainty that a God of love is at home among us.　　　　　　　　Charles Elliot[8]

Heavenly Father, lead me to the desert if that is where I need to be. I will accept your discipline. I will follow your direction. I will rejoice in your deliverance. Because I am your child, I will stay in the desert until your hand leads me home. Amen.

Six

CLAWING YOUR WAY
TO THE BOTTOM

My husband and I learned a great deal while serving New Hope Baptist Church in Mansfield, Texas. Our simple, rural church was filled with some of God's finest people. One day, just after our first son was born, Jim made a pastoral visit to the home of one of our elderly, bedridden members. Puffed with a new dad's pride, Jim was telling the matron the many wonders and talents of our four-week-old, certain that she would be thrilled to hear all about him. The woman lay in her bed, unable to escape, hearing about every burp and bubble. Finally she could take it no longer. Taking my husband's hand, she looked him in the face and said, "Honey, always remember, everyone thinks his crow is the blackest." Jim got the message, quickly prayed for her, and made his exit. I'm sure she was glad to get back to the TV game show she had been watching. Jim and I have never forgotten her words and have found ourselves using that line hundreds of times over the years.

We're all guilty, aren't we? Why should our candidate

win? Because we think our crow is the blackest. Pastors gather at denominational conventions to compare Sunday school enrollments, budgets, and baptism records. Why should our church receive the praise? Because we think our crow is the blackest. Jim and I have made sure we attend the school events and sports programs our sons have participated in and are there when the trophies and awards are given out. We have cheered in the bleachers when our sons played on a team or in the band. Sometimes awards and trophies were won, and sometimes they were lost, but we always thought our crows were the blackest.

Why do we want success and acclaim so much? Where did the concept of reward come from? Why are we motivated by the desire to do more, have more, and be more? The first temptation in the Garden of Eden was rooted in the desire to want more, and this strategy has worked so well that Satan has continued to use it. When God created a perfect world and offered his gift to perfect people, God said that he would always take care of them, that the Garden and all that was in it was theirs, with the exception of just one type of fruit from one type of tree. So what did Satan suggest to Adam and Eve? You can have it—you can be more if you eat it. . . . Why settle for most when you can have it all? A few bites of the apple later, their life spans had been significantly shortened, Adam found himself working in the fields, and Eve experienced the pain women must suffer during childbirth (the single greatest *understatement* in all of Scripture).

Adam and Eve had been able to walk with God in the

Garden and talk with him face-to-face. But when they listened to Satan, they lost that privilege. Adam and Eve wanted to eat the fruit because Satan convinced them that they could be like God. The eternal lesson they learned was that thinking they could *be* like God is what separated them *from* God.

During my college years I worked in a toy store at the local mall. One of my jobs was creating the window displays with the latest toys to draw children into the store. It worked—sometimes too well. One Saturday I watched a family drama unfold. I overheard a small boy outside the store loudly begging his father to take him inside. The boy clutched a dollar bill in his hand, just the amount needed for a new Matchbox car. The father, with a baby in tow, patiently told his older child that they would go into the store after he had fed the baby. The young boy sat next to his father, trying to wait, but temptation got the best of him, and he wandered into the store. His father saw him but didn't stop the boy from leaving. The father with the baby moved to a different bench where he was able to watch his son in the store without being seen.

For several minutes the boy was fascinated by the large display of tiny cars. Then he glanced at the bench in the mall and realized his dad wasn't there. It hit him instantly: He was lost! His wise father watched from a distance until he saw the first tear roll down his son's cheek. The boy didn't see any more of the toy store, and he didn't get his new car that day. His wrong choice came with a consequence. The bigger lesson that day wasn't losing the toy car; it was the feeling of losing his dad.

DON'T ASK FOR THE MOST—ASK FOR THE BEST

Most Christians use the word *lost* to describe people who have never placed their faith in Jesus Christ and received the forgiveness and eternal life provided by his death. These nonbelievers need to ask Jesus to forgive them of their sin and be Lord of their lives. But there is a way for Christians to be lost too—not from the promise of salvation, but from the process of sanctification (being set apart for God). We are lost in this world if we are tempted to believe "our crow is the blackest," that we deserve more and should have more. We wander away from the One who is Lord, content only with the fact that he is Savior. When we disobey our Father, our lives reflect the consequences of our choices rather than the blessings God wants to give us. We are sanctified when we choose to be set apart from the temptations of this world and let God's Holy Spirit work within us.

Jesus confronted two of his disciples who were arguing over which of them should be seated next to Jesus and his glorious throne. James and John thought there was no question that those places were reserved for them, which made the other disciples indignant that they would think such a thing.

Jesus said to them, "You don't know what you are asking!
. . . Are you able to be baptized with the baptism of suffering
I must be baptized with?" Jesus called them together and said,
"You know that the rulers in this world lord it over their people.
. . . But among you it will be different. Whoever wants to be a
leader among you must be your servant, and whoever wants to
be first among you must be the slave of everyone else. For even

the Son of Man came not to be served but to serve others and to give his life as a ransom for many." **Mark 10:38, 42-45**

Why didn't the disciples know what they were asking?

What is the difference between a ruler of this world and a leader of the faith?

John believed he was Jesus' favorite disciple. He was included in the inner circle of disciples with Peter and his brother James. Like many others of his day, John probably believed the Messiah would establish his throne on earth; he wanted an earthly position that he believed would accurately reflect his relationship with Christ. Jesus, however, knew his Kingdom would not be on this earth. He told John that sharing in his glory was asking for suffering on this earth, not a position of respect. John wanted the most coveted spot in the Kingdom. He wanted to be a leader among the disciples. That eventually would be true of John. As an elderly man, he would be persecuted because of his ministry and exiled to the island of Patmos, the Alcatraz of his day.

The priorities of this world encourage us to claw our way to the top in search of the most this life can offer. Jesus teaches us how to claw our way to the bottom . . . in search of the best that he can give.

❧ POINT TO PONDER

Does your life reflect the values of this world or those of Christ?

SEEK TREASURE, NOT TROPHIES

We have a box of trophies and awards in our attic—many of the honors for our sons' accomplishments in baseball, basketball, band, Bible drill, and other activities. Some awards are significant and others are not. But even the important ones don't seem important anymore. Trophies are important at the moment, but only for the moment.

Christians often fall into the trap of doing "good things" that the world notices and rewards. We feel good about receiving attention and acclaim from other people. Society tells us to reach for the stars, climb to the top of the ladder. Often we deceive ourselves into believing that we have a stronger witness based on this visible reputation. Yet Jesus taught his disciples a much different lesson. He said:

> *Watch out! Don't do your good deeds publicly, to be admired by others, for you will lose the reward from your Father in heaven. When you give to someone in need, don't do as the hypocrites do—blowing trumpets in the synagogues and streets to call attention to their acts of charity! I tell you the truth, they have received all the reward they will ever get. But when you give to someone in need, don't let your left hand know what your right hand is doing. Give your gifts in private, and your Father, who sees everything, will reward you.* **Matthew 6:1-4**

A few verses later Jesus tells them,

Don't store up treasures here on earth, where moths eat them and rust destroys them, and where thieves break in and steal. Store your treasures in heaven, where moths and rust cannot destroy, and thieves do not break in and steal. Wherever your treasure is, there the desires of your heart will also be. **Matthew 6:19-21**

What are the differences between "good deeds" done publicly and those done privately?

Why should we be motivated to be "secret servants"?

Why did God set up this system of service? (Matthew 6:21)

The United States has about 6,500 men and women working as Secret Service agents. Their job is to protect and insure the safety of the highest-ranking officials of our government and their families. When a president is considered to be in danger, these highly trained individuals use their bodies as human shields. I read that at Lady Bird Johnson's funeral more than fifty Secret Service agents who had served her family over the years were there. Living in such close proximity to the Johnson family, they had almost become an extension of it. Secret Service professionals do their jobs with neither personal recognition nor public acclaim. In fact, they couldn't do their jobs if they had either of them.

God said his children are to be secret servants. Our job is not to protect a person but to protect our witness. It's easy to be tempted to choose a ministry based on the personal recognition or attention it might bring. If the trophy is large, we might be more likely to volunteer. Scripture teaches us to minister privately, not to seek public reward from people. Our motivation should be for eternal treasure, not temporal trophies. Godly motivation will protect you from becoming busy with the good things this world offers, and will cause you to seek the "God things" you are called to do.

⚏ POINT TO PONDER

Have you earned more treasure or trophies thus far?

SEEK BLESSING MORE THAN APPROVAL

Adam and Eve liked the Garden of Eden. They were happy with what they had, happy with each other, and content with God. When they began to want what they could not have, and thought they deserved to have it all, they sinned. When Adam wanted Eve's approval more than God's blessing, he sinned. Christians want the blessing of God—and God wants to bless them. So what is the problem? Why are there so many times when we feel that God is absent and we are isolated from his presence and power? James, the half brother of Jesus, had an answer.

What is causing the quarrels and fights among you? Don't they come from the evil desires at war within you? You want what you don't have, so you scheme and kill to get it. You are jealous of what others have, but you can't get it, so you fight and wage war to take it away from them. Yet you don't have what you want because you don't ask God for it. And even when you ask, you don't get it because your motives are all wrong—you want only what will give you pleasure. You adulterers! Don't you realize that friendship with the world makes you an enemy of God? I say it again: If you want to be a friend of the world, you make yourself an enemy of God. What do you think the Scriptures mean when they say that the spirit God has placed within us is filled with envy? But he gives us even more grace to stand against such evil desires. As the Scriptures say, "God opposes the proud but favors the humble."

James 4:1-6

Describe the war that is taking place within us.

Why don't we have what we want and get what we want?

What is the sin of adultery in this passage?

What do *you* think the Scriptures mean when they say that "the spirit God has placed within us is filled with envy"?

I admit it. I have always been somewhat of a fashion wannabe, envying the woman who is a size four and has shoes to match every outfit. I, on the other hand, have a long way to go. I was sitting in church one day when I realized that I had on one blue shoe and one black shoe. The shoes that I had nabbed at a sale were identical except for the color. I learned that in the early morning light, black and blue can look remarkably alike. Envy, too, can make things look much different than they actually are.

Human envy can range from trivial things like wanting someone's shoes to dangerous envy that triggers sinful behavior. Over the years my husband and I have counseled several families that were destroyed by a spouse's adultery—a classic example of the grass looking greener in someone else's pasture. In every case, the sin of selfishness was gratified; only later would the spouse who strayed realize that the green grass he or she lusted after turned out to be artificial turf.

Our human spirit is at war with the Holy Spirit that God has given us. God placed his Spirit in you when you were saved, to be your guide, your teacher, his voice. The human spirit's natural tendency is to be gratified by the things of this world that serve its personal desires. The divine Spirit wants to glorify God and serve him and what he desires.

Christians who want to serve God and follow his will

are moved to the front lines of the war of want. "Frontline Christians" are in the heat of the battle in hand-to-hand combat with the enemy. Satan's strategy against you and your ministry is to attack your witness. As Christians, we must examine our personal motivations before even considering to engage Satan in battle. What brought you to the front line? Did you want your peers' approval, or did you long for God's blessing? Winning the war of want will depend on your answer.

POINTS TO PONDER

Who is winning the war of want in your life? Are you more likely to feel victorious if you have received the world's approval or God's blessing?

LIVE WITH DIVINE PURPOSE

You have probably heard the expression, "If you've nothing to aim at, you'll hit it every time." Believers know that God has called us to serve him with humility and will often volunteer for ministries or service opportunities when needed. We want the reward and blessing that we have been taught comes with our choice to volunteer. But so often we want to volunteer on *our* terms. Volunteering is always easier when we commit to those "one time, for one week" service opportunities. They fit nicely into our schedules and we can plan accordingly. So we "aim" at accomplishing as many of those planned and programmed acts of service as we can. The apostle Paul says we are to minister and serve much more frequently than that. In fact, he encourages us to have that attitude toward everything we do.

Work willingly at whatever you do, as though you were working for the Lord rather than for people. Remember that the Lord will give you an inheritance as your reward, and that the Master you are serving is Christ.   **Colossians 3:23-24**

How does Paul define serving the Lord?

When should you expect to be rewarded for your service?

This passage was written to people who were slaves in Paul's society. What are the implications for our lives if Christ is our Master?

When the women of my church want to schedule a big event or program I am usually one of the first people they call. I could delude myself into thinking that the committee needs me to be there in order for an event to be successful. Realistically, my presence is only a fraction of the equation; my position has more impact. It makes sense. If volunteers are needed, who is going to say no to the preacher's wife? No one wants to tell the preacher's wife, "I'm sorry, I can't help with the fall banquet because I need to go to the mall." Well, almost no one. As for me, I am not the best recruiter for volunteers in our church. I believe that members should check with God, not their calendars, to see if they should volunteer (not a popular position when large recruitment is necessary).

Church programs are labeled "service to God," but they don't always turn out that way. Truthfully, so often we see volunteers being praised for all their accomplishments instead of offering praise for God and what *he* has accomplished. Please understand my point. Running a church requires a tremendous amount of volunteer hours and ceaseless energy. But when our motivation for volunteering comes not from God's Spirit but from self-centered motives, God's plan is no longer our plan.

We live in a world that separates our work from the work of God. Can you understand why this idea is not biblical? God wants us to be willing to work at any task in front of us anywhere we are, with the hope of serving and glorifying him through it. Our purpose is to be a witness wherever we go and through whatever we do. Our Christian service cannot be defined by what is programmed or scheduled. God didn't set it up that way. We keep trying to walk on spiritual treadmills, but God has called us to step away from a self-programmed commitment and walk faithfully with him.

❧ POINT TO PONDER

Are you willing to serve God whenever you can, or do you have a desire to serve him whenever he wants?

The temptation to be friends with this world is strong. Getting along with the world around us seems like the best idea. I watched a preacher on TV tell me that God wants me to be successful, influential, and powerful. He said that God wants me to be wealthy and have a life of abundance here on earth—after all he is my Father, and isn't that what a father wants for his child? It sounds great—a lot better than what I read in Scripture.

Jesus said to his disciples, "If any of you wants to be my follower, you must turn from your selfish ways, take up your cross, and follow me. If you try to hang on to your life, you will lose it. But if you give up your life for my sake, you will save it. And what do you benefit if you gain the whole world but lose your own soul? Is anything worth more than your soul?" **Matthew 16:24-26**

Jesus said to be in the world but not of the world. How is that possible? How do we witness to a world if we can't belong in it? I think we start by answering the question Jesus asked. "Is *anything* worth more than your soul?" It's an easy answer to give but a challenging commitment to live. How do you live in this world for the sake of your soul?

It's human nature to seek other people's recognition and rewards. After all, we think our crow is the blackest, our needs matter most, and we deserve to have it all. Keep in mind who made the tempting offer to Adam and Eve and later, to Jesus himself. Your human nature will be at odds with the Spirit that God has given you. How will you be faithful and submit to what God rewards? "Fear of the LORD teaches wisdom; humility precedes honor" (Proverbs 15:33).

Think about what you value. What are you most willing to work for? Are you more likely to earn the world's trophies or the Kingdom's treasure? "Wherever your treasure is, there the desires of your heart will also be" (Matthew 6:21).

This world provides an abundance of amusing, entertaining, and enjoyable opportunities. Christians are not denied the privilege of working hard and enjoying what we earn. The war of want is waged over our priorities and our motives. Jesus said, "No one can serve two masters. For you will hate one and love the other; you will be devoted to one and despise the other. You cannot serve both God and money" (Matthew 6:24).

Clawing our way to the bottom goes against our human nature; the world says we must climb upward to accumulate our rewards. But God tells us, "My thoughts are nothing like your thoughts. . . . And my ways are far beyond anything you could imagine. For just as the heavens are higher than the earth, so my ways are higher than your ways and my thoughts higher than your thoughts" (Isaiah 55:8-9). Jesus left the place of the greatest rewards and humbled himself by coming to earth. His example of humility is what we need to follow. Jesus said, "Take my yoke upon you. Let me teach you, because I am humble and gentle at heart, and you will find rest for your souls" (Matthew 11:29).

🎋 POINT TO PONDER

Has your soul found the rest that Jesus said is available to you?

Someday I will look into that box of trophies in my attic and smile at the good memories they provide. But I pray that I will always remember that trophies are temporal, not everlasting. The award that I will keep forever is the one that my soul yearns for. There is nothing in this world of greater value than hearing my Father tell me, "Well done, Janet. You are a good and faithful servant." I will find that reward and rest for my soul—as I claw my way to the bottom and find the presence of Jesus.

> Better to love God and die unknown than to love the world and be a hero; better to be content with poverty than to die a slave to wealth; better to have taken some risks and lost than to have done nothing and succeeded at it; better to have lost some battles than to have retreated from the war; better to have failed when serving God than to have succeeded when serving the devil. What a tragedy to climb the ladder of success, only to discover that the ladder was leaning against the wrong wall.
>
> Erwin Lutzer[9]

Father God, help us think your thoughts, live like Jesus, and work by the power of the Spirit. May we see the dust that gathers on the trophies of this world and choose eternal rewards instead. Help us, God, to want your blessing more than anything this world can offer. Help us to claw our way to the bottom, so we can serve with Jesus. It is in his name we pray. Amen.

Seven

ARE YOU INFLUENCED OR INSPIRED?

Were you a fan of TV's *The Brady Bunch*? This family sit-com that premiered in 1969 made television history not for its creative humor or its intelligent writing, but because it was one of the first prime-time programs that showed a married couple sleeping together in a double bed. Other popular TV couples like Rob and Laura Petrie and Thurston Howell III and his wife, Lovey, had separate beds.

What a difference a few decades has made! Does anyone on television even believe in getting married anymore? Consider TV programs today. Have you found yourself cheering on characters or actions from a show only to realize that if the same scenario were being played out in real life, you wouldn't possibly condone it? Or maybe you find yourself sanctioning in real life what God would never lead a Christian to support. Are your thoughts and opinions influenced by the *world* to a greater degree than by the *Word*?

Think about the people who strongly influence our society today. How many of them have a Christian influence that is evident? How many have a biblical orientation? Next, think about these questions as they relate to your own life. Who has had a positive influence on you? Have you been taught to be a better person, a better employee, a better parent, or have you been encouraged to be a stronger Christian? Surrounding ourselves with people who provide a good influence in our lives is extremely important, but spiritual strength and growth requires a godly influence.

Finally, who would name *you* as someone who had strongly influenced their lives? From the world's standpoint, you can be a good influence on those around you by offering them your advice or suggestions, based on your personal experiences and firsthand knowledge. From a Christian perspective, however, you can be a godly influence if you pray to be inspired, asking the Spirit of God to speak to another person through you. How many people know Jesus as Lord because they first knew you?

The decline in our society's moral character and the overall acceptance of our current values doesn't seem to surprise many people today. What is surprising is that this viewpoint doesn't *bother* many people today. Christians, in record numbers, are accepting the decline in church growth and the continual decay of society as inevitable. When interviewed, high-profile Christians often blame the government leaders, the media, or schools as being responsible for the negative influence permeating society. Why do Christians blame lost people for being lost? Should we be surprised when non-Christians act in non-Christian ways? Is the problem the presence of negative influences, or is the problem an overwhelming absence of God's Spirit at work in his children?

Jesus said to his disciples, "You are the light of the world—like a city on a hilltop that cannot be hidden. No one lights a lamp and then puts it under a basket. Instead, a lamp is placed on a stand, where it gives light to everyone in the house. In the same way, let your good deeds shine out for all to see, so that everyone will praise your heavenly Father" (Matthew 5:14-16).

The early church emerged from a world that disagreed with its message, often to the point of persecuting and even killing believers. Yet the early church changed the world. Is it time for God's children to once again be the "light of the world" and not allow God's message to be placed "under a basket"? We will only be light when we live as God inspires us to live and avoid the influence of anything less. A. W. Tozer said, "It is not what a man does that determines whether his work is sacred or secular, it is why he does it."[10]

☙ POINTS TO PONDER

Who or what has the greatest influence on your life today? Is it a Christian influence?

CHOOSE A STANDARD FOR TRUTH

My boys learned early in life that Monday through Friday, Mom got first dibs on the television set from 3:00 to 4:00 in the afternoon. I would get them a snack, suggest an activity, pour myself a diet soda, and enjoy my afternoon talk show and its now very famous host. I saw the first national broadcast of this woman's program, and I have seen most of them over the years. I have watched her grow into a powerful voice for women everywhere. She is now considered one of the most influential women in the world.

When her show first aired I was pleased that she would mention God. Over the years, she has changed his name to "her higher power." When the show's topic was abortion, I disagreed with the position she took, but I had counseled women long enough to recognize that many are proabortion because of past abuse or because they themselves have chosen abortion. I hoped that the host would someday grow to a biblical understanding on the subject, and I remained concerned that her opinion would influence others to make a wrong choice. Recently, she did a show on marriage. She has never been married, and she has lived with a man quite openly. The counselor appearing on the show (labeled the "expert") spoke of the problems she had experienced with her marriage that had eventually led to her divorce.

The two of them were discussing that marriage is an outdated institution, completely unnecessary for women because women have achieved a place of power in the world. In essence, women didn't need to rely on a man's income for support. (That is certainly true of the host herself.) I watched in amazement as many of the women in the audience nodded their heads in agreement with the advice they were hearing. I have to admit that the host and her guest voiced a rational argument, but one that is certainly unbiblical.

My greatest frustration with this talk show host is that she has often used a phrase that at first sounds impressive, even intellectual. But if you listen closely, you'll hear her change a well-known phrase with one word. She will often dismiss another person's comment by saying, "That is your *personal truth*." In other words, you are allowed that opinion, but it doesn't have to be mine. She has removed the word *opinion* and inserted the word *truth*. And she has raised an entire generation of women to believe that truth is relative, not absolute. This television personality's influence has been profound, but her inspiration has not been the truth of God. I find it troubling that the Christian women I teach are often satisfied with the apparent truth of her words without questioning their validity.

The world sees this celebrity as a noble person who has done a great deal of good for others. I agree. She has given large sums of money in an effort to improve the lives of many people, showing her great generosity and compassion. Her steadfast commitment to helping others has warmed my heart. I appreciate her for many reasons, but much of the time, I strongly disagree with her message.

Our job as Christians is not to judge her life or her motives. Our job is to be *discerning* when we hear an unbiblical statement that is defined as truth. It is our job to live using God's standard for truth and nothing less.

Our world is constantly influenced to believe in *personal truth*, which is completely different from *perfect truth*. This problem is not new. In fact, the idea that we can choose what to accept as truth has been around since Adam and Eve fell for it. Satan used just enough truth to lure them away from the whole truth.

Satan: "Did God really say you must not eat the fruit from any of the trees in the garden?"

Eve: "Of course we may eat fruit from the trees in the garden. It's only the fruit from the tree in the middle of the garden that we are not allowed to eat."

Satan: "You won't die! God knows that your eyes will be opened as soon as you eat it, and you will be like God, knowing both good and evil."

The woman was convinced. (Based on Genesis 3:1-6)

Study Genesis 3:1-6. What is the truth? What is not?

Why do you think Eve was convinced by Satan?

☸ POINT TO PONDER

How do you determine if something is partial truth or perfect truth?

Satan is called the father of lies, but he also knows the effectiveness of partial truths. Total lies are usually easy to disprove and dismiss. Partial truth takes more effort to think through. People are less likely to examine or worry about things that, on the surface, have the appearance of good. Could that be why we are content to be good, even though we have been called to be godly? The philosophy of our world today appears to be "If a statement contains enough good, then it is good enough." But consider these verses:

All Scripture is inspired by God and is useful to teach us what is true and to make us realize what is wrong in our lives. It corrects us when we are wrong and teaches us to do what is right. God uses it to prepare and equip his people to do every good work. **2 Timothy 3:16-17**

[Jesus said,] "Heaven and earth will disappear, but my words will never disappear." **Matthew 24:35**

Above all, you must realize that no prophecy in Scripture ever came from the prophet's own understanding, or from human initiative. No, those prophets were moved by the Holy Spirit, and they spoke from God. **2 Peter 1:20-21**

Jesus was praying for himself and his disciples just before leaving the Passover table and going to the garden of Gethsemane. In his prayer he said,

Make them holy by your truth; teach them your word, which is truth. **John 17:17**

Referring to the passages above, list the reasons why Scripture should be the Christian standard for truth.

When searching for truth, what have Christians used as substitutes for Scripture?

Why should we be careful to consider the influence of anything besides Scripture?

St. Augustine said, "The faith will totter if the authority of the Holy Scriptures loses its hold on men. We must surrender ourselves to the authority of Holy Scripture, for it can neither mislead nor be misled."[11]

POINTS TO PONDER

Do the Holy Scriptures have a hold on you? Are you surrendered to all that is written in the Bible or are you in danger of being "misled"?

Paul says in his second letter to Timothy:

Work hard so you can present yourself to God and receive his approval. Be a good worker, one who does not need to be ashamed and who correctly explains the word of truth. Avoid worthless, foolish talk that only leads to more godless behavior.

2 Timothy 2:15-16

What will you do to avoid the negative influences that may lead to "godless behavior"?

Why should we work hard to know the Scriptures?

Have you decided to make the Bible your standard of truth?

I don't watch my talk show as often anymore. When I do watch, I listen more closely to what is being said. I don't want to be influenced by someone's "personal truth," only by *the* truth. There are a lot of television shows, movies, and conversations that may fall into the category of "worthless, foolish talk." It's important to watch these programs with spiritual discernment, asking yourself, "Is it truth because someone said it or because God inspired it?"

Most of us will not have as large an audience or the sphere of influence that the host of a television program has. But we still must be intentionally faithful to the people God brings into our lives. He will not hold us accountable for people we couldn't reach, only those that we were given *to* reach. Will you work hard to know the truth, tell the truth, and present yourself to God for his approval? Only his approval will matter eternally.

POINTS TO PONDER

Who has God brought into your sphere of influence? Have you been faithful to the task?

EXAMINE YOUR THOUGHTS

Do you remember the last time you went somewhere quiet because you needed time to think? How do you usually search for the answers you need? This generation is the first one to have access to search engines that practically guarantee a quick answer to almost any question. Research no longer requires wading through volumes of information in search of an answer. Now all that is required is Internet access and a few minutes. Does this mean we have more time to think, or that we have less need to think?

Recently a sports trainer was working with a highly paid professional athlete. The athlete's goal was to improve his focus and raise his batting average. When the trainer was interviewed about his technique, he told the reporter that the average person had two or three thousand thoughts each day. He was trying to help the athlete become so focused on baseball that the number of his thoughts would be reduced to about one thousand per day. I recently learned what this athlete was being paid each year, probably indicating that the trainer has been successful.

The poet Ralph Waldo Emerson says that "A man is what he thinks about all day long."[12] What do you think about all day long? Think about this: Most of us have two or three thousand thoughts a day—and our heavenly Father knows every one of them. How many of your thoughts are directed toward him? King David wrote Psalm 139 poetically explaining God's knowledge of who we are and what we think. The psalm says:

O Lord, you have examined my heart and know everything about me. You know when I sit down or stand up. You know my thoughts even when I'm far away. You see me when I travel and when I rest at home. You know everything I do. You know what I am going to say even before I say it, LORD. You go before me and follow me. You place your hand of blessing on my head. Such knowledge is too wonderful for me, too great for me to understand!   **Psalm 139:1-6**

The fact that God is focused on our thoughts should cause us to want to focus on our thoughts as well. Why are your thoughts so important to God? King David answers that question at the end of the psalm. He writes:

Search me, O God, and know my heart; test me and know my anxious thoughts. Point out anything in me that offends you, and lead me along the path of everlasting life.   **Verses 23-24**

Why does God want to examine your thoughts? Why should you want him to?

In the first century, Corinth was a busy city, bustling with sea trade and world commerce. The Corinthian church was growing and advancing the Kingdom because of its location and ministry. But the society that surrounded the church was beginning to influence the people in the church. Paul wrote his second letter to the Corinthians because the Christians were being influenced by other "teachers" who not only said Paul's teaching was flawed but claimed that their words had the same value as the gospel. Paul addressed the problem by saying:

We are human, but we don't wage war as humans do. We use God's mighty weapons, not worldly weapons, to knock down the

strongholds of human reasoning and to destroy false arguments.
We destroy every proud obstacle that keeps people from knowing
God. We capture their rebellious thoughts and teach them to obey
Christ. And after you have become fully obedient, we will punish
everyone who remains disobedient. **2 Corinthians 10:3-6**

Why are Christians to "wage war" on the ungodly influences of
the world?

Why do we need to address influences that are "obstacles" to
the truth?

What does Paul say to do with any thoughts that rebel against
the truth of God?

⚘ POINT TO PONDER

How can you control influences that cause you to think or
act in ways that oppose God?

I will always be grateful to the friend who showed me
the truth of 2 Corinthians 10:5. I had often been taught that
my outward behavior was crucial to my Christian witness. I
had never been taught that how I acted was actually the "second stage" of my witness. Paul says that we need to take our
thoughts captive and cause them to be obedient to Christ. If

our thoughts are obedient to Christ, then our behavior will likely follow. We have learned to consider our behavior and then act as a Christian should. In Romans 12:2, Paul teaches us to focus on our thoughts so we can *think* like a Christian should and then act accordingly.

God will transform you and your behavior if you allow him to change the way you think. How do you do that? Consider the first part of the verse: "Don't copy the behavior and customs of this world." If your thoughts are more strongly influenced by the world than the inspired voice of God, you will have difficulty being obedient to Christ. How many of your two or three thousand thoughts each day could qualify as a "God thought"? Consider this truth:

"My thoughts are nothing like your thoughts," says the LORD. "And my ways are far beyond anything you could imagine. For just as the heavens are higher than the earth, so my ways are higher than your ways and my thoughts higher than your thoughts." **Isaiah 55:8-9**

What is the difference between a human thought and a God thought?

During Jesus' last moments with his disciples he said:

When the Spirit of truth comes, he will guide you into all truth. He will not speak on his own but will tell you what he has heard. He will tell you about the future. **John 16:13**

Who will speak God thoughts to you?

The times we live in have been described as the age
of information. We have immediate access to the world's
knowledge simply by "logging on" to it. We allow the influence of the world into our home every time we turn the television set on. How can we avoid the inevitable impact this
influence will have? Examine your thoughts and eliminate
any that are contrary to the Word of God. Pray that you will
be determined to obey to Christ.

*Don't let anyone capture you with empty philosophies and
high-sounding nonsense that come from human thinking and
from the spiritual powers of this world, rather than from Christ.
For in Christ lives all the fullness of God in a human body. So
you also are complete through your union with Christ, who is
the head over every ruler and authority.*   **Colossians 2:8-10**

❧ POINTS TO PONDER

**Will you take the time to honestly examine your thoughts and
see if you have been taken captive by influences other than
Christ's? Ask the Holy Spirit to guide you in this process.**

Be aware that a television show or a well-meaning friend
or family member can have a stronger influence on your
thoughts than God. Christians don't intend to follow the
world, but they frequently do. Satan is a roaring lion, seeking to devour our souls, our witnesses, and God's truth. Be

cautious of anything that is only a good influence in your life. Ask yourself if it is *good* or *God*.

CHOOSE INSPIRATION OVER INFLUENCE

Remember the story of Joshua? This young man of great faith was chosen by Moses to be one of the twelve spies to enter the Promised Land and report what he found. When Joshua and Caleb mentioned that they had seen giants, they immediately followed it up by saying that God would help the Israelites defeat them. The other ten spies told the people that they should be afraid of the giants. Those who agreed with the ten spies never entered the Promised Land. Their descendants would take the land, but those who chose influence over inspiration were left to wander in the wilderness. The consequences of listening to influential people can be devastating to your life and to the lives of others. How can you learn to follow the inspiration of God instead? Look at Joshua's words, spoken just before his death, to the Israelites who had followed him into the Promised Land and all the battles that followed:

Fear the LORD and serve him wholeheartedly. Put away forever the idols your ancestors worshiped when they lived beyond the Euphrates River and in Egypt. Serve the LORD alone. But if you refuse to serve the LORD, then choose today whom you will serve. Would you prefer the gods your ancestors served beyond the Euphrates? Or will it be the gods of the Amorites in whose land you now live? But as for me and my family, we will serve the LORD. **Joshua 24:14-15**

Christians need to always be concerned about the choices they make. What is the only acceptable choice that a Christian can make?

In the Joshua passage, how is every choice that is not acceptable described?

The Israelites wanted to follow the Lord. They remembered all that God had done for them, helping defeat their enemies and take the Promised Land for their homes. They remembered the miracles and said, "We will serve the Lord." Joshua heard their conviction and their willingness and responded to it with a warning, the same warning we should hear today. He said,

"You are not able to serve the LORD, for he is a holy and jealous God. He will not forgive your rebellion and your sins. If you abandon the LORD and serve other gods, he will turn against you and destroy you, even though he has been so good to you." But the people answered Joshua, "No, we will serve the LORD!" "You are a witness to your own decision," Joshua said. "You have chosen to serve the LORD." **Joshua 24:19-22**

New Testament Christians must view the passage above in the light of the New Testament truth that the apostle John succinctly states:

If we confess our sins to him, he is faithful and just to forgive us our sins and to cleanse us from all wickedness. If we claim we have not sinned, we are calling God a liar and showing that his word has no place in our hearts. **1 John 1:9-10**

Compare the two passages, then answer the following questions.

What sin must God always judge and discipline?

Why do you think Joshua reminded the people they were a witness to their own decision?

Christians will never be perfect. God doesn't expect us to be sinless. . . . He *wants* us to be sinless. And he gave us his Son so that ultimately we would be. Jesus is the only one who lived a completely sinless life. The rest of us are susceptible to the influence of the prince of this world. Biblical history records the weaknesses of God's people. We live in a fallen world, and we live with our fallen nature. We don't mean to sin—but it will happen.

We need the inspiration of God to strengthen us against the influence of the world. We need to hold each other accountable for our Christian witness. We need to choose— *each day*—to serve the Lord. How many of your two or three thousand daily thoughts will encourage you to serve someone else? How can you live an inspired life?

Remember that God's Word is the truth, the whole truth, and nothing but the truth. So help us God—to ignore what isn't the truth.

Remember to continually examine your thoughts and transform them into God's thoughts. Choose to live intentionally with discernment, as lights brightly shining, as people who reflect the love of Christ to others.

The world has changed a great deal in the last thirty years. What will it look like in another thirty? That will be up to us. Will Christians be influenced by the world or inspired by God's truth in the years to come?

Henri-Frédéric Amiel was a Swiss writer and philosopher who lived in the 1800s. He said, "Truth is not only violated by falsehood; it may be equally outraged by silence."[13] Christians know the truth, and the time has come to speak that truth in love (see Ephesians 4:15). Personal truth is just another way of defining opinion. Perfect truth is defined by the Creator God. You need to choose this day which definition of truth you will follow. Then choose again tomorrow. And may your influence prove that you chose wisely.

Lord and Master, search our hearts and know our thoughts. Show us what you oppose and lead us to your perfect truth. And may our witness prove we believe it.

Eight

DO YOU SPEND OR
INVEST YOUR TIME?

God created this world with a sun, a moon, and four changing seasons. The tides ebb and flow, the air warms and cools, and mirrors reflect our physical changes with each passing year. The great equalizer of this world transcends culture, wealth, and gender. It is unaffected by money spent or even efforts to control it. That great equalizer is the passage of time.

In a few weeks we will take our younger son, Craig, to college. I will cry as Jim and I drive home, and when we arrive and I walk into the house, almost everything about my daily life will be different from that time on. The moment is both sad and exciting; above all, the moment is right. I have reached the end of one season of life and will move into the next. I have few regrets about the past and carry a wealth of wonderful memories. I look forward with faith to what God has planned for the months and years to come.

One of the things I'll miss the most is the halftime program at the high school football games. Both of my sons were in the marching band, and I would sit anxiously in those bleachers waiting for the first half of the game to end so "the real show" could begin. Jim and I proudly watched our boys play their trumpets, marching in perfect formation. I suspect I will still attend a few football games, but halftime won't be the same for me, because the tallest trumpet players whose faces are so familiar to me will no longer be there. Time has moved on, and so has that music.

Every day we awake to the rhythm of God's will, a playlist he has specifically written for us. We can request a change in the music, but God makes the final selection. Occasionally he includes a song that is more difficult to master. Like a member of a band, we need to follow the music, or we misstep. God is the conductor of life, and the rhythm and pace of the music is his decision, not ours. The symphony of our lives has a beginning and an end. But the end of one song on earth is simply the promise of the next in heaven.

I'm certain that the apostle John would rather have been home in Ephesus, instead of exiled on the island of Patmos in the Mediterranean Sea. Jesus came to John in a cave on that island and gave him a vision of heaven, instructing John to write it down. If John had not been isolated on Patmos, he may not have been able to record what the future holds in store for believers. He wrote:

I saw no temple in the city, for the Lord God Almighty and the Lamb are its temple. And the city has no need of sun or moon, for the glory of God illuminates the city, and the Lamb is its light. The nations will walk in its light, and the kings of the world will enter the city in all their glory. Its gates will never be closed at the end of day because there is no night there. And all the nations will bring their glory and honor into the city.

Revelation 21:22-26

Think of it. Time will cease to exist in heaven because all things there are eternal. Time is simply a tool in God's hand for those of us on earth. God knew we would need constant reminders that this life is finite, that every day and season on earth can be measured. God established precise measurements of time's passage so that we would remember the *way* we choose to *use* our time has eternal effects. Time can be spent on things that give temporary benefits, or time can be invested in things that have eternal reward.

SEE TIME AS AN OPPORTUNITY

Time management became a buzzword in the eighties. And big purses were all the fashion rage. The two actually worked in tandem. Why? Women needed big purses to carry their time-management notebooks around. During that decade, almost every church retreat and business conference offered at least one workshop on time management. I admit that I bought a notebook and took the class. But I ran into trouble when I realized I didn't have a big purse—I had a big diaper bag permanently attached to my shoulder.

At that time in my life, I needed diapers, bottles, toys, and small sandwich bags filled with Cheerios. Those practical items made my days far easier to manage than a book with addresses, phone numbers, and a detailed agenda. My detailed agenda was feeding babies, changing babies, and keeping the babies mildly entertained throughout the day. Who needs a book for that?

The idea, however, of an organizer, guaranteed to transform my chaotic life to a well-managed life, seemed like a dream come true. I just wasn't able to convince my one-year-old that he would have to wait to eat or have his diaper changed until his "penciled-in time slot" arrived. Truthfully, that thought is no more absurd than the times we look at God and tell him we don't have time to listen to or obey him.

Time-management classes teach us that if we organize our time, we will have more free time to spend. Has that happened to you? Do you find yourself with countless hours of free time because you have become more organized? We can schedule almost every minute of our lives, but more than likely at the end of the day that schedule changes.

When you asked Jesus to be your Lord, you gave up the right to plan your own life. You are no longer in charge of your time. That actually is a reason to be thankful, isn't it? It's just difficult to remember that our life-management planners were turned in when God gave us his Holy Spirit to be our guide.

I'm a strong believer in organization and living a self-controlled life. But I need to remember that when I see the word "self-control" in Scripture, it is better translated "God-controlled self."

God knows that I like a clean and orderly house, which is why he gave me a husband and two sons. Julian of

Norwich writes, "God did not say, 'You shall not be tempest-tossed, you shall not be work-weary, you shall not be discomforted.' But he said, 'You shall not be overcome.'"[14] Although my younger son has tested me to the max in the area of tidiness, I have not been "overcome." Actually, the real miracle (and probably true of most mothers in this situation) is that Craig and I are both still alive and love each other. There were days during his childhood when I was convinced that he had been switched at birth. How could anyone with my genes live—even seem to thrive—in such chaos! I'm already planning on writing an apology letter to his future wife!

Truthfully, the Lord has often used my children to teach me the important lesson of perspective. I used to think a spotless house was a necessity rather than a priority. One night Craig came to our bedroom, asking for some help. He was "talking" to a friend online who had some serious faith questions. Craig led this young man to Christ the Savior that night, probably surrounded by a week's worth of dirty laundry on his bedroom floor. I'm glad he wasn't cleaning his room instead of taking that time for his friend! I wonder how many ministry opportunities I have missed because I thought I should be cleaning instead of doing something else—perhaps something with eternal value.

How many times has God wanted to interrupt your schedule with an opportunity for ministry? In my experience *most* of God's ministry is an interruption to whatever you have planned. The phone rings as you are walking out the door. A person stops you in a parking lot. Someone wants to speak to you after church. Maybe you notice a person who is hurting, and your heart knows God is sending you to his or her side. Is God able to interrupt your schedule? Do you *expect* him to?

Peter preached to the multicultural crowd in Jerusalem after his Pentecost experience. Scripture says that he spoke to them for a long time, explaining their need for forgiveness and salvation. Acts 2:41 says, "Those who believed what Peter said were baptized and added to the church that day—about 3,000 in all." Those people became a community of believers, an excellent definition for a church. God would provide the apostles appointments for ministry from that time on. Acts 3 reveals one such appointment.

Peter and John went to the Temple one afternoon to take part in the three o'clock prayer service. As they approached the Temple, a man lame from birth was being carried in. Each day he was put beside the Temple gate, the one called the Beautiful Gate, so he could beg from the people going into the Temple. When he saw Peter and John about to enter, he asked them for some money. **Acts 3:1-3**

> The Temple referred to in this passage is the same Temple that Jesus and the apostles would have visited frequently, including each day of the Passion Week. Reread the passage. How often was the beggar at the Temple gate? Why is that fact significant?

What were Peter and John doing at the Temple?

What do these verses teach you about appointments for ministry?

Peter and John looked at him intently, and Peter said, "Look at us!" The lame man looked at them eagerly, expecting some money. But Peter said, "I don't have any silver or gold for you. But I'll give you what I have. In the name of Jesus Christ the Nazarene, get up and walk!" **Acts 3:4-6**

Luke, the author of Acts, points out that Peter and John "looked" at the lame man. Why do you think Luke used the Greek word *atenizo* that translates "looked intently"?

The man wanted money, but the apostles didn't have any money to give. What can we learn about ministry from this passage?

✄ POINT TO PONDER

What should we consider when God doesn't give us what we ask for?

Then Peter took the lame man by the right hand and helped him up. And as he did, the man's feet and ankles were instantly healed and strengthened. He jumped up, stood on his feet, and began to walk! Then, walking, leaping, and praising God, he went into the Temple with them. **Acts 3:7-8**

In this story of Peter's encounter with the lame man, what did Peter do?

What did God do?

What did the lame man do?

How does this passage define an appointment for ministry?

All the people saw him walking and heard him praising God. When they realized he was the lame beggar they had seen so often at the Beautiful Gate, they were absolutely astounded! They all rushed out in amazement to Solomon's Colonnade, where the man was holding tightly to Peter and John. **Acts 3:9-11**

Why is it crucial to carry out "God-arranged appointments" for ministry?

Peter saw his opportunity and addressed the crowd. "People of Israel," he said, "what is so surprising about this? And why stare at us as though we had made this man walk by our own power or godliness? For it is the God of Abraham, Isaac, and Jacob—the God of all our ancestors—who has brought glory to his servant Jesus by doing this."　　**Acts 3:12-13**

This was a moment of opportunity for Peter. How could he have used this time to benefit himself? What did he do instead?

⚘ POINTS TO PONDER

Whose ministry do you have great respect for? Should you?

Time is an opportunity. Time can be managed, manipulated, misused, or missed. Or we can make it available to the Spirit of God. For a long time I did not understand why Jesus told his disciples that after he ascended to heaven, they would do even greater things than he did (John 14:12). But I came to realize that Jesus' earthly ministry of three years was limited by his humanity; he could only be in one place at a time. After Jesus' ascension, the Holy Spirit continued the earthly ministry of Christ through his indwelling power given to everyone who believed. When Peter extended his hand to the lame man, in reality the lame man was taking the hand of Jesus . . . and then he could walk. Peter and John knew it was Jesus' miracle; they had simply been the conduits for his power. The apostles made certain that everyone listening knew whose miracle it was too.

Jesus may have walked past this lame man several times during his three years of ministry. But God had reserved this appointment for ministry for Peter and John when they were going about their daily business. What does that mean for you and me today? Not every ministry need is your opportunity, only those arranged in God's timing. For Peter and John, God's timing arranged the miraculous healing of the lame man so that the apostles could establish and watch the Christian church grow in Jerusalem. God's appointments for ministry have greater purpose than we usually know in the moment. But they are always an opportunity to use our time for God's glory.

Is your time so managed and scheduled that God cannot interrupt it? Resolve to make yourself available for his appointments. Are you so busy with your ministry that you don't have time for God's ministry? Time is an opportunity. Welcome each day as a chance to walk with the Spirit, available to his call. These are the appointments that must never be missed.

TIME CAN BE REDEEMED

My husband and I love to lead and attend silent retreats, and consequently when we travel we seek out monasteries. The moment we arrive, we sense the reverence of a place that has been intentionally set aside for the purpose of seeking God. Sometimes I wish I could live there all the time. But my home is in a busy neighborhood, in a busy community, and I serve a busy church. We have Sunday school programs, church programs, charitable organizations' programs, and holiday programs. We have missions meetings, committee meetings, counseling meetings, and program-planning meetings.

In addition, I still have to complete the inevitable household chores that come up daily. There are definitely days when I have complained to the Lord, "I am weary in well-doing." But I love his answer: "Don't be" (Galatians 6:9). Unless you have chosen a monastic lifestyle, you have to actively find ways to allow God to redeem your daily life for his good purposes.

Do you remember S&H Green Stamps? Between the 1930s and the early 1980s, many retailers rewarded shoppers with actual green stamps based on how much they purchased. The stamps were pasted in booklets and then redeemed for consumer items at a redemption center. One summer my sisters and I set our sights on the Deluxe Monopoly game. We had a lot of shopping and a lot of eating to do if we were going to have enough stamps! After each shopping trip, we carefully pasted our "green gold" into the booklets. Then one day it happened—we filled the last page! It didn't seem like Mom could drive fast enough to that redemption center. We left with a new Deluxe Monopoly game that day; I still have it. The effort to get the game made it much more valuable to us. We found a way to redeem money for more than just groceries.

You have to work, attend meetings, participate in PTA events, watch your children play sports, and fulfill countless other time commitments. You live in the real world. How could God "redeem" those time commitments for his glory? Is it possible that your ordinary moments could lead to extraordinary occasions God has set aside for you?

I love the story of Queen Esther. The book of Esther is a fascinating account of the Israelites who remained in Persia when the others had returned to the Promised Land. I am always touched by the lessons taught in this book. One of my life verses is found in Esther, chapter 4, verse 14.

The Israelites had been taken captive by the Persians and were living under their rule. The king, dissatisfied with his queen, Vashti, requested other young women be brought to his palace. Esther was one of the young women chosen from the crowds. Esther found favor with those she met, including the king, and this young Jewish woman was given the title of queen. Haman, a royal official, was given the highest position in the kingdom, and the people were ordered to kneel down and pay honor to him. Esther's cousin Mordecai was a devout Jew and refused to kneel before a man. Haman, enraged by Mordecai's choice, tricked the king into signing a decree that put the entire Jewish population's lives in danger. At her cousin's urging, Esther faced the task of speaking to the king on her people's behalf. For the moment Esther was safe, her Jewish lineage hidden. But she had not been summoned by the king, so she was in danger of death if she entered, unbidden, into his presence. There are many reasons she should have refused to go. When she hesitated, her cousin Mordecai sent this message:

Don't think for a moment that because you're in the palace you will escape when all other Jews are killed. If you keep quiet at a time like this, deliverance and relief for the Jews will arise from some other place, but you and your relatives will die. Who knows if perhaps you were made queen for just such a time as this? **Esther 4:13-14**

Why did Mordecai believe that Esther was given the position of queen?

Why might you have been placed in your positions of leadership or influence?

🐚 POINT TO PONDER

Where might God have placed you "for just such a time as this"?

Paul was teaching the church in Ephesus to live by the Spirit's power. He writes:

So be careful how you live. Don't live like fools, but like those who are wise. Make the most of every opportunity in these evil days. Don't act thoughtlessly, but understand what the Lord wants you to do. **Ephesians 5:15-17**

How would Paul teach you to handle the time commitments you have?

What would he caution you to do before accepting an obligation?

Scripture instructs Christians to live *in* the world but not be *of* it. We are the light of the world and the salt of the earth. We need to live and be seen as godly influences for the world. We have to spend time getting to know the world because we may be the reason someone in the world will come to know the Lord. God can redeem the moments spent in our daily lives by telling his thoughtful children what he wants them to do with the time. Paul would say, "Be wise! Make the most of every opportunity."

It comes down to your awareness. Can you reach the grocery item that is too high for someone? Do you know the name of the person ringing up your purchase? At the next meeting you attend, does one person have tears in her eyes or seem angry about something? Do you know who at the office just went through a divorce and may need someone to talk to? Have you met your newest neighbors and answered any of their questions about schools, garbage collection, or community activities? Do you know anyone who is sick and needs help with the kids? or who just lost his or her job? Be thoughtful. Be wise. Then remember . . . maybe God has placed you in that person's path for "such a time as this." Give God a chance to "redeem" your time for his glory. Living thoughtfully is a call from God. But you will reap the joy and blessings.

INVEST YOUR TIME IN SERVICE TO CHRIST

My husband and I have money deducted from every paycheck and deposited into an annuity. Although we know the money is there and it's ours, it doesn't benefit our life today. The annuity is just a promise that our future will be secure. One day we will have our nest egg, but not any time soon. Sometimes ministry feels that way. It can cost us time, sometimes even money. We can serve God and not see any immediate benefits. In fact, we can occasionally lose some of this world's reward because we choose to give of our time in ministry. We know about the promised reward, but it is our investment for the future, not for today. There is difficulty choosing to serve when eternal investments usually don't have immediate payoffs and occasionally carry some risk.

In Matthew 25, Jesus was speaking to his disciples about the final judgment. He would soon enter Jerusalem and begin his journey to the Cross. He knew his disciples would face difficult times after his death, but Jesus wanted them to draw strength and comfort from the promise of eternal reward. Jesus told them:

But when the Son of Man comes in his glory, and all the angels with him, then he will sit upon his glorious throne. All the nations will be gathered in his presence, and he will separate the people as a shepherd separates the sheep from the goats. He will place the sheep at his right hand and the goats at his left. Then the King will say to those on his right, "Come, you who are blessed by my Father, inherit the Kingdom prepared for you from the creation of the world. For I was hungry, and you fed me. I was thirsty, and you gave me a drink. I was a stranger, and you invited me into your home. I was naked, and you gave me clothing. I was sick, and you cared for me. I was in prison, and you visited me." Then these righteous ones will reply, "Lord, when did we ever see you hungry and feed you? Or thirsty and give you something to drink? Or a stranger and show you hospitality? Or naked and give you clothing? When did we ever see you sick or in prison and visit you?" And the King will say, "I tell you the truth, when you did it to one of the least of these my brothers and sisters, you were doing it to me!" **Matthew 25:31-40**

What service does Jesus say the righteous will be rewarded for?

How much time have you invested in that service?

Why do you think the righteous Jesus spoke of were unaware of their ministry to him?

When Ryan and Craig were young we often took them to someone's house for lunch after church. They knew that if our hostess had made peas, they'd be expected to eat peas. Occasionally one of them would stomp his foot right before we were ready to leave for our lunch invitation and say, "I'm not going!" On those occasions I would take his face in my hands, make him look at me, and say, "I know you don't want to go. But would you do it for me?"

There are days I picture God doing the same thing with me. Sometimes I do grow weary with our ministry. I wish I could just stomp my foot and say, "I don't want to go!" I find strength in visualizing Jesus taking my face in his hands and saying, "Would you do it for me?" Somehow, his hands holding my face and his gentle yet convicting eyes put all of my wants and supposed needs in a different perspective. I cannot imagine looking into his face or seeing his scarred hands and then saying anything but, "Of course I will do it for you, Jesus!" But to be honest, I am still human and there are times when I hope Jesus isn't "serving peas"!

My husband and I have been in pastoral ministry for more than twenty-five years. These years of both ministering to people and being privileged to see the results of their subsequent ministries bring two verses of Scripture to mind. They are verses that almost every Christian knows but not enough of us understand.

Don't be misled—you cannot mock the justice of God. You will always harvest what you plant. Those who live only to satisfy their own sinful nature will harvest decay and death from that sinful nature. But those who live to please the Spirit will harvest everlasting life from the Spirit.   **Galatians 6:7-8**

The truth of these verses is visible to my husband and me every day. We see people feeling abandoned because they have been in the hospital and no one called. We visit grieving family members who don't know who to ask to be the pallbearers at a relative's funeral. We talk to people who think they don't fit in with the church or that no one cares about them. We try to calm the people who are outraged by decisions made at meetings they never attended. I want to tell each of them the verses from Galatians, but I don't want to hurt them with the truth these verses contain. I hope that by teaching this verse passage, God's truth will help someone later.

Interestingly enough, Paul follows this hard truth with a huge encouragement: "So let's not get tired of doing what is good. At just the right time we will reap a harvest of blessing if we don't give up" (verse 9). What a joy to know that each time we choose to persevere and serve, we can be the hands, feet, and voice bringing the love of Jesus to someone's life!

It is always true when it comes to eternal reward—we reap what we sow. But so often that truth shows up in our earthly relationships as well. We sit with people whose hospital rooms make us sneeze from the abundance of flowers. They are exhausted because their friends constantly come to visit. Yet others count the days before they can go home without a friendly knock on their door. Should the church reach out? Absolutely. We are the hands and feet of Christ.

It is a chance to serve him. There are moments in this life that reveal what kind of seeds you are planting with the life you lead. From time to time, stop what you're doing and evaluate your harvest.

> Do you take advantage of the ministry appointments God brings into your life? Remember: No one ever forgets the person who led him or her to the Lord.

> Do you redeem daily moments for his glory? God will lead you through the ordinary moments of life and then call you to the extraordinary moments "for such a time as this."

> Do you invest in ministries that allow you to serve Jesus? Have you already received some of your reward or is it eternally invested?

> Do you understand that your life on earth and your eternal life will be blessed by the seeds of service that you have planted?

> If you serve in a ministry to which you've been called, have you grown weary? Why? Look Jesus in the face, and do it for him.

Someday we will live in the city John saw and described in the book of Revelation. Time will cease to exist, and everything we know and see will be eternal. We won't see a sun or a moon. There won't be a temple. Jesus will be the only light we will ever need, and every moment will be to worship him. Until then, the sun will measure the day and the moon will measure the night. The seasons will progress and so will our lives. Each day holds the promise of reward if we spend our time as God has called us to. William Barclay wrote, "The only way to get our values right is to see, not the beginning, but the end of the way, to see things, not in the light of time, but in the light of eternity."[15]

May we all spend the days we have left investing in our eternal annuity. As the famous Baptist preacher R. G. Lee used to say, "It will be payday, someday."

Lord Jesus, may we look at our hands and see yours. May the words we speak be authored by your Spirit. May we walk where you want to go and stay as long as you want to stay. And may we do it for your sake and yours alone.

Nine

FIGHT THE PHARISEE WITHIN

Beware: If you have been a Christian for at least a year, you have Pharisee potential. Take it from a "paid Christian" like myself, there is a Pharisee inside most of God's children—especially those of us on the payroll. Differentiating between legalism and pure obedience is difficult. The greater challenge, however, is admitting that the struggle exists.

Church attendance and Bible study are essential to spiritual growth. If you attend worship on Sunday, study the Bible, and do all the other "measurable" things associated with spirituality, you could be a Pharisee and not even know it. For those of us who have the title of teacher or minister of the gospel, we carry the additional burden of needing to speak or preach on the world's schedule, which may not be in tune with our own. The crowd arrives expectantly and a message must be delivered. Times like that can produce the Pharisee in us. We have to meet the responsibility of service, and as a result, we rely on our own ability and strength instead of God's.

None of us intend to become Pharisees. This metamorphosis happens when we've learned how to *act* like a Christian. We know how to respond to adversity, how to speak to people's needs, and how to look genuine while we do it. Slowly, we learn how to handle our Christian witness ourselves. People expect us to behave a certain way, so we choose to meet their expectations. Our witness and ministry develop into a performance motivated by what we know and those we need to impress. The process of learning to act like a Christian can hinder us from allowing the Holy Spirit to guide us in becoming more Christlike. Honestly, we are less likely to seek God when we assume we already know his answers.

Sermons and Bible studies are filled with lessons about the Pharisees. We know this group of men tried to discredit the ministry of Jesus. When they were unsuccessful, they sought to destroy him and his movement. We classify these men as evil and jealous of Christ's ministry. In movies, they wear dark hooded robes. They have small, shifty eyes, their expressions foreboding behind their long beards. They shout with loud, caustic voices filled with hatred. Jesus referred to the Pharisees as hypocrites and a brood of vipers.

I have often wondered how the people of the first century could have been persuaded to accept the Pharisees' demands to crucify Jesus. The crowds *did* follow those leaders. Who were the Pharisees, and why were they able to lead the people to God while lacking the ability to recognize him for themselves even when he stood in their midst? We need to understand the reasons why the Pharisees acted and thought as they did. The same weaknesses that blinded the Pharisees can exist in you and me today.

HINDER YOUR HYPOCRISY

One excuse typically made by people who don't want to attend church is, "The church is full of hypocrites." I try to gently respond, "Our church isn't full yet; we would love to make room for you, too." People often have wrong expectations of those who attend church. Each of us is infected with hypocrisy; therefore, each of us will sometimes be a hypocrite. What is hypocrisy? Why did Jesus say the Pharisees were "hypocrites"?

When people are labeled hypocrites today, they consider this a slanderous or negative judgment on their character. When Jesus first used the term in Scripture, he intended it to be an analogy for the behavior of the Pharisees. Later, he used the word *hypocrite* to define the person who did not have a genuine spiritual life and witness.

The word *hypokrites* was commonly used in Greek literature and in the first-century vernacular. The word simply referred to a person who played a part on the stage. A *hypokrites* was an actor. Actors usually wore masks and imitated someone or something they were not. Women were banned from the stage, so men assumed their roles. Behind his mask, an actor could represent an animal, a king—even a god or demon. Jesus first used the word meaning "hypocrite" in the Sermon on the Mount. He was describing those who *acted* like righteous people but had wrong motives for their actions.

Watch out! Don't do your good deeds publicly, to be admired by others, for you will lose the reward from your Father in heaven. When you give to someone in need, don't do as the hypocrites do—blowing trumpets in the synagogues and streets to call attention to their acts of charity! I tell you the truth, they have received all the reward they will ever get. But when you give to someone in need, don't let your left hand know what your right hand is doing. Give your gifts in private, and your Father, who sees everything, will reward you. **Matthew 6:1-4**

What is the primary motive behind those who do good deeds publicly?

What is their reward?

How can you gain eternal reward?

This passage is sobering for people who serve in ministry. Does Jesus mean that our entire ministry should be done incognito? Should we never again thank a church committee for their service or acknowledge people for their ministry? The intent of this passage is crucial. It is important to understand that Jesus was talking about a person's motivation for ministry.

Eternal reward belongs to people who teach Sunday school, not because they want a title or a position "up front," but because they want to be used by the Holy Spirit to teach God's truth. But a person may agree to serve because she wants to belong to a certain group and have her name listed in a program. Jesus' sermon teaches that the program, pasted in a scrapbook, is her only reward.

Jesus requires each of us to examine our motives. Our "God deeds" must be done for his sake and his glory. Our reward comes from the knowledge that we are usable by his Spirit and are able to be the hands and feet of Christ in someone's life. The great, eternal privilege of service is the opportunity to allow Christ to minister through us. Taking credit for ministry would be like a weatherperson taking credit for a beautiful day. Meteorologists can forecast, but they can never create the weather.

Jesus continued to discuss ministerial motives in his Sermon on the Mount when he said:

When you pray, don't be like the hypocrites who love to pray publicly on street corners and in the synagogues where everyone can see them. I tell you the truth, that is all the reward they will ever get. But when you pray, go away by yourself, shut the door behind you, and pray to your Father in private. Then your Father, who sees everything, will reward you. When you pray, don't babble on and on as people of other religions do. They think their prayers are answered merely by repeating their words again and again. Don't be like them, for your Father knows exactly what you need even before you ask him!

Matthew 6:5-8

What is a hypocrite's motive for prayer?

Consider the verses carefully. Why should you pray?

One evening at our first church, we were paid an unexpected visit by a former pastor. We had been warned previously that this man's message and ministry were more than a little self-serving. When he asked my husband for the opportunity to say a few words to the congregation, Jim did not want to give him the platform but also didn't want to be unkind. So Jim asked the former pastor to close the service in prayer, thinking that would circumvent the situation. We bowed our heads, and for the next ten minutes we listened to the man use his prayer to raise funds for his "ministry." When he finally said Amen I was pretty sure I detected smoke coming from my husband's ears!

I detest prayers that are prayed because someone wants to make an announcement or voice a personal opinion. Those prayers are insulting to God and I believe bring judgment on the person praying. Prayer is a gift of God, given so that we can fellowship with our Father. God gave us prayer so that we could enter the Holy of Holies and talk with the Creator of the universe. Prayer is an opportunity to voice our needs, but even more, prayer is a chance to hear what God wants to tell us. We know what we want but God knows what we need.

A hypocrite imitates a prayer because he has an ulterior purpose for his prayer other than fellowship with the Father. Jesus taught that we should find a closet and pray in order to have a conversation with God. "When you pray, don't be like the hypocrites. . . ." Every time you bow your head to pray aloud remember that your audience is the God of the universe, no one else.

POINT TO PONDER

Do you pray like Jesus taught or like the Pharisees?

Later, Jesus taught the crowd to watch out for the hypocrites who judge others. He said:

Do not judge others, and you will not be judged. For you will be treated as you treat others. The standard you use in judging is the standard by which you will be judged. And why worry about a speck in your friend's eye when you have a log in your own? How can you think of saying to your friend, "Let me help you get rid of that speck in your eye," when you can't see past the log in your own eye? Hypocrite! First get rid of the log in your own eye; then you will see well enough to deal with the speck in your friend's eye. Don't waste what is holy on people who are unholy. Don't throw your pearls to pigs! They will trample the pearls, then turn and attack you. **Matthew 7:1-6**

Describe the person whom Jesus is calling a hypocrite in this passage.

Jesus does not say we shouldn't confront people with their sin. This passage teaches how we need to do it.

> What is your standard for judging? Note: It is the same standard by which you will be judged.

> What should you do before you confront people with their sin?

> When should you not confront a person?

🕮 POINTS TO PONDER

Think about the last time you talked to a friend about his or her sin and the person gladly accepted your help. Why were your words helpful instead of judgmental?

In the next verses, Jesus gives an excellent lesson on how not to be hypocritical when judging others, and how to avoid "throwing pearls to pigs!" Jesus taught:

Keep on asking, and you will receive what you ask for. Keep on seeking, and you will find. Keep on knocking, and the door will be opened to you. For everyone who asks, receives. Everyone who seeks, finds. And to everyone who knocks, the door will be opened. You parents—if your children ask for a loaf of bread, do you give them a stone instead? Or if they ask for a fish, do you give them a snake? Of course not! So if you sinful people know how to give good gifts to your children, how much more will your heavenly Father give good gifts to those who ask him. Do to others whatever you would like them to do to you. This is the essence of all that is taught in the law and the prophets. **Matthew 7:7-12**

When you want to genuinely counsel someone, how can you know that the moment is right and your motive is pure?

When you pray for or give counsel to someone, whose help are you actually giving in that moment?

What is "the essence of all that is taught in the law and the prophets"? Why is this statement the preventative for hypocrisy in our witness?

The single most important ministry lesson I have learned is "I will never know how to minister on my own." People come to the pastor or pastor's wife for counsel or help with their needs. Concerned church members may seek help with a problem they see in the congregation. The single greatest mistake my husband and I can make—and have made—is to think we know how to handle the situation. I have developed a habit that minimizes my ministry mistakes. It is my "help me, God" prayer. When someone is expressing a concern or need, I am listening and praying, *Help me, God*, as they speak. I try not to talk to someone about a wrong they have committed, unless I have already prayed for God's help to know if and when to confront them. Every person's situation is unique, so it doesn't matter if I have given counsel before in a similar situation. I wouldn't know what to do unless I have prayed. There may be sins in my own life that would make my words hypocritical unless I have prayed first. I rely on God's direction through prayer. The "help me, God" prayer causes me to focus my thoughts on the Holy Spirit and allow him to take the lead.

There is a great deal of self-directed and world-directed ministry today, where critical mistakes are being made. I believe that most mistakes happen when God's people have not sincerely and fervently prayed. We may have pure motives, but unless we also seek God's council, we will lack his answer. God has said, "My thoughts are not your thoughts and my ways are not your ways." Jesus said, "Keep on asking, keep on seeking, keep on knocking" until you have God's answers to offer.

You have good gifts to utilize, but God wants you to give his gifts to that person so much more. Do you want others to judge and help you by their standards? Or do you want to be judged and helped by the perfect standard that can only come from God? Don't give others *your* counsel. Pray until you can give them God's. Only his word will be perfect, without hypocrisy.

The church is full of hypocrites because the church is full of human beings. Human nature will always want attention and gratification. Human nature is flawed and will produce ungodly acts. The only nature we have that is not tainted with hypocrisy is God's nature through the Holy Spirit. The Pharisees acted as though they were pure, but they were not. Jesus called them hypocrites because he could see immediately that it was their human nature, not God, controlling their actions. They wore a mask of righteousness to cover up their humanity. I certainly understand Jesus' anger toward the ministry of the Pharisees. But I am immediately humbled: These men had access to God in the flesh, but they did not have his indwelling Spirit. How much more accountable to God am I, having received his indwelling power and presence?

Why do Christians make the same mistakes the Pharisees did? Often we don't want people to know who we really are because they might think less of Jesus. Thinking we are doing God a favor, we give ourselves permission to act like Pharisees. We need to keep the Pharisees within us from wearing the mask of a Christian. Such a mask will never hide the fact that we are flawed human beings. What can we do to be certain that we don't imitate the Pharisees?

First, you must learn to live honestly. People see behind masks; the only person who is truly fooled is the one looking back at you in the mirror. If you have sinned, confess it. If you have wronged someone, go and admit it to that person. If you have lied, say so. You are imperfect until you die and are made perfect in heaven. Don't expect perfection from yourself, and don't allow others to expect it in you. That is an honest witness.

Second, you must strengthen your witness. Sanctification is the process of being made holy. It begins by first admitting the sin in your life and then omitting the sin. Jesus told the woman who had been caught in adultery and the Pharisees who wanted to stone her that anyone who was sinless could throw the first stone. Each was forced to face his or her sins. Later, Jesus told the woman that no one had condemned her, himself included, but added that she was to go home and "sin no more." (John 8:1-11) Being human is not an excuse for sin. When God saved you, the Holy Spirit took up residence in your life. You carry within you the presence and power of God. Because God is unable to sin, every moment he is in control will be a sinless moment in your life. You asked him to be your Savior—keep asking him to be your Lord.

Finally, pray without ceasing. Learn to breathe prayers throughout your day, in the everyday moments of your life. A friend of mine recently lost her spouse and was struggling with the various changes his death had caused. She told me that she was usually fine during the day but the evenings were difficult. "I sometimes turn to comment on something or ask a question and realize that his chair is empty," she said. "He won't answer." More than anything else it was those moments of companionship that she missed.

I think our prayer relationship with God is a lot like that. There are times when we stop all that we are doing to "talk." But much of our conversation with him comes during the day, when we just turn our thoughts to heaven and make a comment, ask a question, or offer our praise. And God will always answer. I breathe air because it is necessary to live. I breathe prayers because it is necessary if I want to live for God.

Every day we see people who don't know how to get to heaven and don't realize they should care. Not all of them are ready to hear the gospel and not all of them are yours to tell. You cannot be called to ministry and you cannot be sanctified for ministry unless you live prayerfully. You are not being a hypocrite when you seek God's help. Quite the contrary. Asking for his help is the only sure way to battle the sin of hypocrisy in our lives.

DON'T FOLLOW THE PHARISEES

Why did the crowds seeing Jesus on trial join with the Pharisees and shout "crucify him"? How could they? The Pharisees had given their lives to the study of God's Word. As a group, they had defied the Roman government when they were asked to acknowledge Herod as a god. The Pharisees prayed more, spent more time in the Temple, and proudly positioned themselves as "examples to follow" to the people who wanted to know God. Outwardly, they lived the most righteous, obedient lives humanly possible. The Pharisees were good people in many ways, but Jesus said they weren't godly. The crowds couldn't tell the difference. Can you?

What does a godly person look like? How can you make that judgment call without disobeying the Scripture that teaches us not to judge? The best answer that I have ever heard came from my friends E. K. and Sheila Bailey. They have taught many of us that "Christians have to be fruit inspectors." Jesus said the same thing in his Sermon on the Mount. He said:

Beware of false prophets who come disguised as harmless sheep but are really vicious wolves. You can identify them by their fruit, that is, by the way they act. Can you pick grapes from thornbushes, or figs from thistles? A good tree produces good fruit, and a bad tree produces bad fruit. A good tree can't produce bad fruit, and a bad tree can't produce good fruit. So every tree that does not produce good fruit is chopped down and thrown into the fire. Yes, just as you can identify a tree by its fruit, so you can identify people by their actions.

Matthew 7:15-20

How is a false prophet disguised in this passage? What does that description mean?

What is a person's "fruit"?

What do you think is the difference between judging a person and identifying them?

This warning from Jesus is critical. Every church has both sheep and wolves sitting in the pews. The wolves dress and sound just like the sheep, but they wear a disguise of faithfulness. Paul addressed the problem in his second letter to the Corinthians. He wrote,

> *These people are false apostles. They are deceitful workers who disguise themselves as apostles of Christ. But I am not surprised! Even Satan disguises himself as an angel of light. So it is no wonder that his servants also disguise themselves as servants of righteousness. In the end they will get the punishment their wicked deeds deserve.* **2 Corinthians 11:13-15**

How do you identify the wolves? More importantly, how do you keep yourself from becoming one? The answer to both questions is by prayerfully becoming a fruit inspector.

When I speak, I love to use this illustration. I set two apples on the podium. One of the apples is real and the other is artificial. No one in the audience can distinguish the difference until I ask someone to come up and inspect the fruit. Close up, the differences are unmistakable. Wolves dressed like sheep look almost identical to real sheep. The only way we can detect the difference is by looking closely.

Then I hold up both apples and describe them. The artificial fruit is perfect in appearance. There are no bruises or breaks in the skin. Often the artificial apple appears to be in better shape than the real one. My artificial apple doesn't have a stem (some might). It was never attached to a tree and so it never needed one. A real apple is created because it was attached to a tree that produces an apple. Artificial fruit can sit in a bowl and look good for years. With a little dusting, this plastic fruit will maintain its fresh and "tasty" appearance. Real fruit doesn't need maintenance for the best appearance—it requires sustenance.

An artificial witness can often look better than a genuine witness. The artificial witness seems flawless and is "stem free." It makes sense because a false witness is manufactured, not grown. A real witness cannot be manufactured; God himself must create him. What strengthens and sustains your witness: you or God?

But the real difference between my two apples is the weight. One apple is much lighter than the other because it is hollow. The same is true with a person's faith. Just like people who reach for artificial fruit when they are hungry and walk away disappointed and unsatisfied, many people lead Christian lives that are hollow, unable to benefit anyone. Only real fruit can feed people when they are hungry. Seeds can only be found in the center of a real apple. Real apples produce other apples; real Christians produce other Christians. Does your witness result in the fruit of people coming to know Jesus as Lord and Savior of their lives?

What does it mean to be a fruit inspector? It means you look closely at a person's life to identify whether that person is a sheep, or a wolf disguised as a sheep. You won't be able to tell unless you have the chance to inspect his or her life. Most wolves carefully limit their exposure to spiritual situations. When surrounded by real sheep, their disguise is easier to notice. Wolves might have the appearance of faith, but they are unable to produce the fruit of a godly witness. In

truth, they often feed on the sheep. Significantly, wolves produce other wolves, not sheep.

Jesus finished the Sermon on the Mount by saying:

*"Not everyone who calls out to me, 'Lord! Lord!' will enter
the Kingdom of Heaven. Only those who actually do the will of
my Father in heaven will enter. On judgment day many will
say to me, 'Lord! Lord! We prophesied in your name and cast
out demons in your name and performed many miracles in your
name.' But I will reply, 'I never knew you. Get away from me,
you who break God's laws.' Anyone who listens to my teaching
and follows it is wise, like a person who builds a house on solid
rock. Though the rain comes in torrents and the floodwaters rise
and the winds beat against that house, it won't collapse because
it is built on bedrock. But anyone who hears my teaching and
ignores it is foolish, like a person who builds a house on sand.
When the rains and floods come and the winds beat against
that house, it will collapse with a mighty crash." When Jesus
had finished saying these things, the crowds were amazed at his
teaching, for he taught with real authority—quite unlike their
teachers of religious law.* **Matthew 7:21-29**

Jesus said, "I am the way, the truth, and the life. No one can
come to the Father except through me" (John 14:6). Salvation
comes through placing your faith in the only Savior, Jesus
Christ. The Sermon on the Mount reveals that not all who call
Jesus Lord have made him Lord. How does Jesus identify the
false witness, the one he "never knew"?

Who are the foolish people and who are the wise people?

What is the difference between performance and obedience?

🐚 POINT TO PONDER

Is your Christian witness better described as a good perfor-mance or as godly obedience?

Paul was in prison and knew he would soon die when he wrote his second epistle to Timothy. He wanted to warn Timothy to be careful and cautious with the people who were in the church but not of the Kingdom. He wrote:

You should know this, Timothy, that in the last days there will be very difficult times. For people will love only themselves and their money. . . . They will consider nothing sacred. . . . They will be cruel and hate what is good. They will betray their friends, be reckless, be puffed up with pride, and love pleasure rather than God. They will act religious, but they will reject the power that could make them godly. Stay away from people like that! **2 Timothy 3:1-5**

The book of Second Timothy was probably written almost forty years after Jesus preached his Sermon on the Mount. Paul's warning in this passage isn't directed at the Jewish Pharisees; his warning is about the people who claim to be Christians, and even some who are Christians. Describe the people who only "act" religious.

Look carefully at the verses. What does it take for a person to be godly?

FIGHT THE PHARISEE WITHIN

This chapter addresses a tough subject and can be disconcerting to read. Most of us have done things which Scripture condemns. We look at our past and admit that it is anything but perfect. Those of us who have been in the church for a significant length of time have occasionally allowed the Pharisee within to surface. There have been days, and may still be days, when our witness is not real but becomes an act of hypocrisy. At some point, all of us have followed leaders instead of following the Lord. Some of us have even been those leaders.

Know that God's grace is sufficient for every sin you have committed because the blood of Jesus was shed for every one of our weaknesses. But be confident: You have been given everything you need to fight the Pharisee within in your life and ministry through God's perfect Holy Spirit.

In the world's eyes, the Pharisees were good men. Some were even considered great men. Jesus said they were a "brood of vipers" and hypocrites. Unless you learn to be a "fruit inspector," quite possibly you will follow a leader instead of the Lord. The consequences of that choice will affect your eternal reward and possibly other people's rewards as well. Remember Paul's words: "Stay away from people like that!"

Do you need to spend some time with the Father so you can evaluate your witness? Every time I teach a lesson about the Pharisees I am reminded of my potential to be just like them. Most Easter seasons I can see myself in the crowd shouting, "Crucify him!" But the Cross reminds me that I will one day be in the crowd that shouts praises to the Lord with the saints and the angels for all eternity. Until then, I have been given the power to fight the Pharisee within and choose to be godly instead. I have also been given forgiveness for the times that I have retreated from the battle. You have, too. The famous preacher Billy Sunday once said, "Hypocrites in the church? Yes, and in the lodge, and at home. Don't hunt through the church for a hypocrite. Go home and look in the glass. Hypocrites? Yes. See that you make the number one less."

Dear Father, I now know it wasn't just the Pharisees who crucified your Son. I did too. Forgive me, Lord, for causing you to suffer. Forgive me, Lord, for flaunting the hypocrisy of a manufactured witness instead of reaching for the power to be a witness who is godly. Help me identify the wolves around me but join the flock of sheep. I want to throw out my masks so that you can easily recognize me when I get to heaven. Amen.

Ten

SIMPLIFIED AND READY TO SERVE

As I look around at the rooms of my house, I see this chapter illustrated in each cluttered corner. I like my surroundings to be neat and organized, but today that would be impossible. Everywhere I look I see a pile of stuff. In fact, it looks like the local bed-and-bath store crashed a truck into my house, spilling the store's inventory all over my floor.

Tomorrow I will help my older son, a college senior, fix up his new room at school. Two days later Jim and I will move our younger son into the freshman dorm at his university. He has been anticipating this moment for a long time. Next week, at home, I will clean my sons' rooms, knowing they will stay clean until Thanksgiving. It doesn't seem possible that in two short days the chaos that surrounds me will be replaced with silence. Right at this moment, organization doesn't seem like all it's cracked up to be. I've been told that the "empty nest" has some real benefits. I'm sure that is true, but I don't see them just now.

I've been a full-time mom for more than twenty years. I

have no idea what I will do with the extra time that I have available to me. If I'm not careful, I know that the extra moments will be filled quickly. I will try to be prayerfully quiet and "practice what I preach." If I don't intentionally seek God, I will find ways to fill my new schedule with my own plans instead of offering my time to the Lord for his direction.

Times of transition are inevitable and potentially powerful. The different stages of life mark significant times of change. But change also occurs with a new job choice, a new service opportunity, or sometimes because it's time for something different. Tragedy can bring unwelcome change, often accompanied by painful decisions. Change can be many things, but above all, change is guaranteed because it is a natural part of this world. God allows or causes times of transition and he can make them work for the good—as long as we choose to be called to his purpose (Romans 8:28). A Christian usually faces these transitional times by praying more frequently and more earnestly seeking the will of God. Our great comfort in any transition is that God is ever present, ready to illuminate his path for our life. Our great distress is that God rarely seems to be in as much of a hurry to shine that light as we are to see it. Could it possibly be that the Lord lingers because he enjoys the extra time we choose to spend with him during the seasons of change? Scripture says, "Come close to God, and God will come close to you" (James 4:8).

I think I have hugged my boys fifty times this week. I want to be near them now because I know they won't be here next week. My love for Ryan and Craig reminds me why God orchestrates changes resulting in our desire to draw near to him. Sometimes I forget how much we are loved and how much God yearns to be with us.

I am looking forward to this next season of my life even as I grieve the one just past. My duties as a full-time mom are complete, so I should be able to focus on my relationship with God in a new way. I will still think of my boys and pray for them every day, but I won't be doing their laundry or making extra trips to the grocery store. My life has been simplified, and I will do my best to keep it that way.

What one word best describes your lifestyle? I have known very few people, myself included, who would use the word *simple* to indicate how they live each day. More often than not, I hear words like *frantic, hurried, fractured, distracted, stressed,* or *complicated.* For many Christians, church responsibilities fragment their time even more. Is this the lifestyle that God really designed for us?

DECIDE TO CARRY A LIGHTER LOAD

Every time I ask a group about the most significant hindrance to their spiritual life the number one response is, "I am just too busy." It doesn't matter if I am talking to men or women, young or old, wealthy or poor, employed or unemployed. The answer invariably is "I know I need to serve God more, I just can't seem to find the time." Imagine standing before the Father explaining *that* excuse to him. We need to simplify our lives so no excuses will be necessary.

I love Oswald Chamber's devotional, *My Utmost for His*

Highest. First published in 1935, this devotional has been "raising" God's children ever since. The August 5th entry says:

> A Christian is someone who trusts in the knowledge and the wisdom of God, not in his own abilities. If we have a purpose of our own, it destroys the simplicity and the calm, relaxed pace which should be characteristic of the children of God.[16]

Is this simplicity and pace characteristic of your life? There will always be times when life becomes frenzied and overscheduled. But those times need to be rare in a Christian's life. Frenzy tends to bring out the human nature in God's children, not the presence and peace of God.

The pace of this world continues to escalate. Unless we choose to go at God's pace, we risk moving at the world's speed that keeps us busy, but more than likely will not help us to be godly. How can you know if you have complicated your life beyond the will and expectations of God? Jesus gave the answer to his disciples. He said:

> *Come to me, all of you who are weary and carry heavy burdens, and I will give you rest. Take my yoke upon you. Let me teach you, because I am humble and gentle at heart, and you will find rest for your souls. For my yoke is easy to bear, and the burden I give you is light.* **Matthew 11:28-30**

What is promised to those who take their burdens to Jesus?

Jesus does not give us his yoke; he asks us to *take* it upon our-selves. Why is that verb significant?

Why should Jesus' instruction to his disciples be ours as well?

The yoke of Jesus is light and not a burden. How is this fact helpful in evaluating your schedule choices?

Even if your life is far from modeling simplicity, consider making it your goal. As human beings we will make human decisions. But with God's help, we can lay down the world's burdens and walk under the yoke of Jesus which keeps us on course with God's plan so we don't stray from his bless-ing. Your life and ministry is a field to plow, but it will be less of a challenge if Jesus has provided the yoke and is hold-ing the reins.

Jesus won't chase you down and force his yoke on you. You will need to volunteer to take it and place it on yourself. You can easily determine whether or not you are too busy doing things that God didn't intend for your life. If you are buckling under the weight of your schedule and you find yourself tired of everything, you are wearing the wrong yoke. As quickly as possible, lay it down and take up the one Jesus will give you.

Oswald Chambers was right. Living life for our own purposes does destroy the calm, relaxed pace that should characterize our Christian life. But what a powerful witness you would be if you were calm and relaxed in this hurried, distracted world. The yoke of Jesus is easy and his burden is light. Are you carrying anything else?

✥ POINT TO PONDER

What burdens do you need to lay down as quickly as possible?

DECIDE TO FORGO YOUR IDEAS IN FAVOR OF GOD'S IDEAS

A simplified life is easier to talk about than to live. It always has been. In 1 Chronicles, we read about a major turning point for King David. Gathering together all the leaders of Israel, he knew the time had come to step away from the throne and hand over authority to his son, Solomon. David's words to the leaders of that day are relevant to us today.

The crowd of distinguished people had gathered in Jerusalem. Everyone present knew King David was going to make a significant announcement. David understood the magnitude of the situation and chose his words carefully. Scripture says:

> *David rose to his feet and said: "My brothers and my people! It was my desire to build a temple where the Ark of the LORD's Covenant, God's footstool, could rest permanently. I made the necessary preparations for building it, but God said to me, 'You must not build a temple to honor my name, for you are a warrior and have shed much blood.'"* **1 Chronicles 28:2-3**

What had David wanted to accomplish during his reign?

With that goal in mind, how had he spent his time?

What kept David from achieving his goal?

How does this passage define the difference between a good idea and a God idea?

When people are about to retire or enter another phase of their life, they often evaluate where they've been, what they've experienced, etc. Think about some of the significant moments from David's life story. What characteristics did Samuel, the last judge of Israel, see in David that made him know that among all of Jesse's sons, this youngest child was to be king? Was it the same confidence Saul saw in the young shepherd boy when he laid aside the king's armor and approached Goliath with just his slingshot? That confidence would turn to arrogance later in David's life, culminating in getting what he demanded (Bathsheba) no matter what the cost. The cost was great, and David would forever live with the consequences of his choice. But King David was a man after God's own heart (Acts 13:22) and by the end of his life, God's heart was what mattered most.

For most of his reign, David wanted to build a temple to house the Ark of the Covenant, Israel's most prized possession. The Ark held the two tablets of the Covenant and was kept in the Holy of Holies, where it was called the seat of God. The Ark indicated the presence of God on this earth. The king wanted to build a place of worship for the people to bow before the presence of the God that he loved so much. In 1 Chronicles 28 the exact plans are recorded—down to the last details which God gave David for the structure, the contents, and even the amount of gold needed to complete the Temple. David made all the preparations, and then God said, "Your son Solomon will build my Temple and its courtyards, for I have chosen him as my son, and I will be his father" (verse 6). That had to be a difficult thing for David to process and accept. David would have to step back from his goal in order to be obedient to God.

Our lives are simplified when we understand that our ministry is designed and ordered by the will of God. There are times when he calls us to step back from our own ideas and goals so that someone else can take our place. Our human nature struggles with the realization that we might have done all the work only to see someone else receive the glory. But isn't it like God to protect us from ourselves! We actually complicate our lives when we choose to carry an entire burden so we don't have to share the glory. The glory belongs to God first and foremost. Are you willing to simplify your life by sacrificing your good ideas in order to accept God's?

DECIDE TO DO YOUR PART AND ALLOW OTHERS TO DO THEIRS

Who are the people you quietly admire? Not necessarily the people who have impressed you the most and possibly not the people you would try to emulate. Who are the people that come to mind in your reflective moments? You may never have spoken to these people and you might not even know their names, but you respect them. My heroes are often people who go unnoticed by many in the church. I often say that when I die I hope God builds my mansion somewhere close to their estates. There is a man from our church in Atlanta who came early and left late almost every time the doors were open. He was a behind-the-scenes person who made sure the microphones were turned on before the service and that they were put away when the event ended. My family receives a card from him on each holiday, simply signed with his name. Luther is one of my heroes.

At another church there was a woman who prepared her Sunday school room on Saturday, making sure it was ready when the two- and three-year-olds arrived. She didn't just teach the children, she loved each of them, and made each of them feel that church was a wonderful place to be. Kathleen is one of my heroes. Another man from that church went downtown each evening to make sure "the boys," his homeless friends, had a sandwich to eat or a blanket to stay warm. Rip is one of my heroes.

There are so many names that I could mention, and I have been blessed to know all of them. They were people who loved the Lord and faithfully served him. They didn't think of what they did as work; it was their passion. They never sought recognition, but I saw and deeply respected their less conspicuous contributions to the church and the Kingdom. I wish I had told them how I felt a little more often.

Who are the people in your life that you quietly admire? Would you be a similar hero on someone's list?

Relinquishing his throne, David said to his son Solomon:

Be strong and courageous, and do the work. Don't be afraid or discouraged, for the LORD God, my God, is with you. He will not fail you or forsake you. He will see to it that all the work related to the Temple of the LORD is finished correctly. The various divisions of priests and Levites will serve in the Temple of God. Others with skills of every kind will volunteer, and the officials and the entire nation are at your command. **1 Chronicles 28:20-21**

What did David define as Solomon's responsibility?

Whose job was it to make sure the job was done correctly?

Who else was involved in the project?

Ultimately, the Temple would be built because many people offered their talents. Why is this an important model for simplified service?

Our Christian lives grow complicated and unbalanced when we find ourselves doing work we were not called to do. Possibly we have chosen a task to which God did not call us; often we choose to fill a job because someone else failed to assume his or her responsibility. Paul taught the church:

In his grace, God has given us different gifts for doing certain things well. So if God has given you the ability to prophesy, speak out with as much faith as God has given you. If your gift is serving others, serve them well. If you are a teacher, teach well. If your gift is to encourage others, be encouraging. If it is giving, give generously. If God has given you leadership ability, take the responsibility seriously. And if you have a gift for showing kindness to others, do it gladly. **Romans 12:6-8**

God requires his children to serve him. Your ability to serve is your gift from God. In what ways has God gifted you to serve his Kingdom?

Our gifts are to be used with a high standard of Christian character. Why is such integrity crucial?

God, in his grace, gave you his gift(s) for service. Why should you eagerly desire to use them for his glory?

✥ POINTS TO PONDER

Do you know your spiritual gift(s)? There is a helpful tool in the appendix of this book which can help you determine how God may have gifted you for service.

Don't you love to give that perfect gift to enhance your friend or loved one's life? So does God. When you became a Christian, the Father gave you unique gifts to enable you to serve his Kingdom and bring reward and blessing to your life.

Jesus told his disciples, "I tell you the truth, anyone who believes in me will do the same works I have done, and even greater works, because I am going to be with the Father" (John 14:12). The Holy Spirit indwells the life of every Christian. How many places in the world is the love, the ministry, and the power of Christ at work today? Just think of it: You and I are the continued ministry of Christ in our world today, through the gifts of the Holy Spirit. Do you allow Christ to minister through you?

Your life will be greatly simplified by knowing your spiritual gift(s). Most of the time, your gift will help you define your call. I once saw a man walk across a large arena on his hands. He could stop and pick up various items and he could turn, hop, and even dance on his hands. We all applauded his unique ability. He was able to do great things while walking on his hands. But even a small child could outrun him in a race. As Christians we tend to struggle and complicate our lives because we are trying to function outside our God-given gifts. When we attempt to accomplish ministry in our own strength, we are walking on our hands. We can get the job done, but not easily or as well. When you function in your giftedness, you function in the power of God. We can learn to "walk on our hands," but that isn't what God made hands to do.

The church has been defined as the body of Christ. Each part needs to function as it was designed to operate. Functioning according to God's design is how the church becomes the hands, feet, and voice of Jesus in our world. No one is particularly *impressed* when a person uses his feet to walk, and no one should be impressed when you minister through your gift. Why? Because that's what you were made to do. God made our feet to walk and run; it's his creative ability that is most impressive. God made you to function in your gift.

When you do, you too will be one of those quiet servants who understands that there is no glory for you in your gift; you're simply doing what you were made to do. You'll experience great blessing, because you have been the presence of Jesus to others. Learn what your spiritual gift is and then minister, allowing Jesus to work through you. Your life will be greatly simplified if you will learn to walk on your feet instead of your hands.

DECIDE TO SIMPLIFY YOUR LIFE

We took our boys to their college campuses and helped them get settled in their rooms. Finally, the moment I had been dreading arrived—we had to say good-bye. Most change requires a moment of decision. When Jim asked me to marry him, I had to decide what my answer would be (it was one of my easier decisions). When the boys were born we had to decide what we would name them. We have made decisions about our jobs, our lifestyle, and our service to God and others. Before we became Christians there was a time when we had to decide to ask Jesus to be our Lord and Savior. And every day since, we decide whether or not to live according to his plan. Most of life consists of the decisions we make and the consequences from those decisions.

You will need to make some resolutions if you want to lead a simplified life of service to God. Your choices will depend on your stage of life, your current responsibilities, and primarily on your relationship to Jesus as Lord. Every spiritual commitment requires the strength and leadership of God. How does Scripture guide you towards a simplified life of service?

Study this Book of Instruction continually. Meditate on it day and night so you will be sure to obey everything written in it. Only then will you prosper and succeed in all you do. **Joshua 1:8**

According to Scripture, what is your path to prosperity and success?

What decisions must be made in order to achieve both?

*But forget [the past]—it is nothing compared to what I
am going to do. For I am about to do something new. See, I
have already begun! Do you not see it? I will make a pathway
through the wilderness. I will create rivers in the dry wasteland.*

Isaiah 43:18-19

What decision might be necessary for you to make in order to
simplify your life and walk along God's path?

*And so, dear brothers and sisters, I plead with you to give
your bodies to God because of all he has done for you. Let them
be a living and holy sacrifice—the kind he will find acceptable.
This is truly the way to worship him. Don't copy the behavior
and customs of this world, but let God transform you into a new
person by changing the way you think. Then you will learn to
know God's will for you, which is good and pleasing and perfect.*

Romans 12:1-2

List the decisions you will need to make if you want to know
God's will.

How would making these decisions simplify your life?

Look here, you who say, "Today or tomorrow we are going to a certain town and will stay there a year. We will do business there and make a profit." How do you know what your life will be like tomorrow? Your life is like the morning fog—it's here a little while, then it's gone. What you ought to say is, "If the Lord wants us to, we will live and do this or that." Otherwise you are boasting about your own plans, and all such boasting is evil. Remember, it is sin to know what you ought to do and then not do it. **James 4:13-17**

Why is it a mistake to make decisions apart from God's counsel?

What is the definition of "sin" in the verse above?

I pray that your love will overflow more and more, and that you will keep on growing in knowledge and understanding. For I want you to understand what really matters, so that you may live pure and blameless lives until the day of Christ's return. May you always be filled with the fruit of your salvation—the righteous character produced in your life by Jesus Christ—for this will bring much glory and praise to God. **Philippians 1:9-11**

How does Scripture describe a simplified life of service?

What do you need to do to choose this life?

I always feel a twinge in my soul when I watch a classic movie or television show that portrays a lifestyle set in a simpler time. The front door of a house is unlocked and the screen door frequently swings open and shut as children and neighbors come and go. The front porch boasts rocking chairs and a table set with iced tea or lemonade. The fences are waist high so everyone can easily converse or wave to each other. Neighbors know each other and can be called on in times of need.

Are those visions of a time gone by or do they symbolize a time when people had a higher standard for living? I don't want to accept the passing of a simpler time; I want to know how that simplicity can be restored. I believe it will begin when God's people once again embrace the lifestyle described in Scripture.

We need to study continually the Word of God and know that the Bible is perfect truth. When we meditate on Scripture throughout the day, the decisions we make are influenced by the Creator God. Our choices become easy when we have God's answers.

Let's embrace the changes that God brings to our lives

and move forward with his direction. If God wants to do a new thing in our lives, why would we want to hang on to the old? If God wants to simplify our lives, will we gladly change? What are "front porches" and "neighborhoods" supposed to look like today? How would yours change if you allowed God to be the architect?

The prince of this world wants to influence our appearance, but children of God should look like their Dad. Satan wants to dress us and accessorize our life with doubt and fear. He pressures us to work harder so that we can have more. God wants to transform us from the inside so that our mind, body, and soul become a reflection of him. When he makes us over, we are able to think like him. When we think like him, we are able to know what his will is. And his will is always perfect.

Make a point to schedule your plans in pencil because you may need to erase them. We only think we know what is best for our lives. Always remember that God knows the complete picture and is incapable of error. Is your life complicated by your plans to the point that you have no time for his? Trust his perfect plan instead of your well-intended one.

Finally, remember what matters most is that you live with the righteous character of Jesus Christ. He indwells you through the Spirit so that each day you can glorify God by allowing Jesus to minister through you. Grow in your knowledge and understanding of Christ and love others as Jesus would love them. You are a gifted child of God—true success is achieved when others admire the fact that you quietly remind them of your "Dad."

I had a hard time leaving my boys at college and coming home to an empty house, but that change was both inevitable and right. Each morning I pray that they are growing up to be the men God has called them to be. I pray that they will live God's plan for their lives instead of embracing the world's agenda. I pray that they will become like the quiet heroes I so admire. I pray that they will simply live like children of the King. I will try to embrace anything God will require of them to simply lead godly lives.

Erwin Lutzer is a pastor and a teacher who describes the simplicity of Jesus in a way that should characterize our lives as well:

> Jesus knew where he had come from, why he was here, and what he was supposed to accomplish. He came down from heaven, not to do his own will, but the will of the Father. That determination controlled every decision he made. As a result he was not distracted with trivia. He was never in a hurry, for he knew his Father would not give a task without the time to do it. Christ was not driven by crises, feeling he must heal everyone in Israel. He could say, "It is finished," even when many people were still bound by demands and twisted by disease. What mattered ultimately was not the number of people healed or fed, but whether the Father's will was being done. His clearly defined goals simplified his decisions.[17]

Lord God, define my goals and give me the wisdom to live the simplified life of a servant. I am tired of living the frantic pace required to achieve what this world calls success. May I move along the path you have provided, holding fast to your hand, until I am safely and peacefully home. May my choices show the world that I want to grow up to be "just like my Dad." I love you and I am proud to be your child.

Conclusion

Solomon said, "Here now is my final conclusion: Fear God and obey his commands, for this is everyone's duty" (Ecclesiastes 12:13). King Solomon wrote an excellent definition for what it means to be godly. The world will try to convince you that being "good" is good enough. God reminds you that he has a higher standard for your life. He wants you to be godly. Solomon said, "This is everyone's duty." You will fear God and want to obey his laws when you understand that God is, that he always has been, and he will always be, the great "I Am."

> When you ask God to help you defeat temptation, his answer is "I Am."
>
> When you ask God to speak to you, his answer is "I Am."
>
> When you ask God to heal your soul, his answer is "I Am."
>
> When you ask God to inspire your choices, his answer is "I Am."
>
> When you ask God to give you his priorities, his answer is "I Am."

When you ask God to bring you out of the desert, his
answer is "I Am."

When you ask God to make you a humble servant, his
answer is "I Am."

When you ask God to use your time for the Kingdom,
his answer is "I Am."

When you ask God to protect you from self-sufficiency,
his answer is "I Am."

When you ask God to bless you with a simplified life,
his answer is "I Am."

God with his powerful love and perfect grace wants to be
the great "I Am" in our lives. But though he created us in his
image, we choose the degree to which we live in obedience
to his will. The first step toward godliness is made when you
know God, through his Son and through his Spirit. Every step
that follows can draw you closer to the Lord. Choose to walk
his path, holding his powerful right hand. God said, *"I will
strengthen you and help you. I will uphold you with my victorious
right hand"* (Isaiah 41:10). Whose hand are you holding? Who
is your source of strength and your constant guide?

A godly person will reach up to find the presence of
God, then reach out and be that godly presence in the lives
of others. Live in such a way that you are the tangible reality of the existence of God. There is no greater blessing in
this world than to be known as a child of the King of kings.
Then, when you bow your head and pray, "I want you to be
proud of me," your Father will answer and say, "I Am."

APPENDIX

Give thanks to the LORD and proclaim his greatness. Let the whole world know what he has done. Sing to him; yes, sing his praises. Tell everyone about his wonderful deeds. Exult in his holy name; rejoice, you who worship the LORD. Search for the LORD and for his strength; continually seek him. Remember the wonders he has performed, his miracles, and the rulings he has given. (Psalm 105:1-5)

Life is a "search for the Lord." It is impossible to live a godly life unless you continually seek him and live with his strength. The Lord wants you to remember any lesson that has drawn you closer to him. Spend as much time as possible with "the Teacher." Reading the Bible is good, but it is better to *study* God's word until you understand it. Ask the Holy Spirit to guide you each time you study the truth of Scripture. Then pray for the wisdom to apply that truth to your own life.

I've included some additional study ideas in this appendix that might strengthen you for this journey we call life. May the Lord bless your desire to "seek him" and "remember the wonders he has performed, his miracles, and the rulings he has given." Dwight L. Moody once said, "I never saw a useful Christian who was not a student of the Bible."[18] Let's choose to be useful.

Fighting the Battle against Temptation

Jesus found his disciples asleep in the garden of Gethsemane. They probably had not intended to fall asleep, but they were tired and unaware of the magnitude of the situation. Christians want to be godly, but we grow tired from the effort and content with the apathy the world allows. We can easily "fall asleep" because we, like the disciples before us, don't understand the magnitude of the situation. The words Jesus spoke to Peter that night speak to us today. He said, "Couldn't you watch with me even one hour? Keep watch and pray, so that you will not give in to temptation. For the spirit is willing, but the body is weak!" (Mark 14:37-38).

What does Jesus tell Peter he needs to do to battle temptation?

Why is the battle difficult at times?

Years later Peter used similar words to warn the early church and encourage them to continue to live for God. He wrote, "Stay alert! Watch out for your great enemy, the devil. He prowls around like a roaring lion, looking for someone to devour. Stand firm against him, and be strong in your faith" (1 Peter 5:8-9).

Why is it dangerous to grow apathetic about your relationship with God? What is your source of strength?

Are you "alert" or apathetic?

The Business of Bible Study

The Bible is called the "Word of God." The Bible is the voice of God. How often do you listen to him? There are some valuable tools that make studying the Bible much easier and more effective.

Invest in a good study Bible.

When you know the background of a passage you can understand what it meant to the original audience. When you understand what the passage meant, you will understand what it means today. Find a study Bible authored by theologians from many denominations who contributed from their particular area of expertise. (That information is usually listed at the front of a study Bible.) If you needed heart surgery, you wouldn't go to an eye doctor. You'd find the best heart surgeon you could. Consider using the same criteria for your spiritual health.

Find a good Bible study group.

Accountability and fellowship happen when Christians come together to study God's word. Hint: Find a Bible study group that spends more time in study than in fellowship.

Pray before you open God's Word.

The Holy Spirit is your most important teacher. Ask him to speak to you and guide you while you study. The Word of God is your daily bread. Don't skip your meal.

Write down what you learn.

We took notes in school if we wanted an A.

Read fewer books about the Bible and more of the Bible.

(Don't tell my publisher I just said that!)

Obey his voice.

I have never known God to make suggestions.

Share what you have learned.

You may be the only source of Scripture some people ever read.

Learn to Seek Silence and Solitude

I think everyone should attend at least one silent retreat a year. I lead silent retreats just so I can go! The following are some guidelines to help you embrace the gift of silence. Feel free to use them—and plan a retreat for yourself and others.

- Find a retreat center that is affordable enough for everyone to have a room of his or her own. Catholic monasteries are a good place to start. Sometimes we just borrow the church on a Saturday and look for quiet places to pray.
- Tell those attending to pack comfortable clothes and leave behind their connections to the outside world—cell phones, pagers, clocks, reading materials, and especially their schedules.
- Meet together as a group and discuss the schedule and any housekeeping rules for the facility. Answer questions or concerns ahead of time so that it won't be necessary to break the silence.
- Make sure there is a way of calling participants to times of prayer, Scripture reading, or group directives.
- Provide Scripture, meditative readings, and quotations on the subjects of silence, peace, prayer, and contemplation. My favorite authors on these subjects are Henri Nouwen, Richard Foster, Mother Teresa, A. W. Tozer, and Thomas Merton.
- Plan to eat together, but do not speak during meals. Bring quiet instrumental hymns and Christian music to play during that time. The quiet feels a little odd at first, but later there will be a tangible companionship in silence.
- Direct the participants to begin their first moments of silence in a time of personal confession. Provide Scriptures that focus on God's forgiveness and healing. It is much easier to spend time with God when you have reconciled with him.
- Release all expectations for the retreat. I have attended many such retreats and found each one to be a unique experience. There are times when God will reveal himself in a powerful way. There are other times when the greatest experience has been the quiet rest and peace that comes from having

walked with God in silent companionship. The only real
goal of a silent retreat is to be still and know that he is God.
Everything else is a bonus.

Smile and greet each other with a wave, but remain silent.
Extended times of listening are rare in this world. Embrace
the fact that we can speak to God and never utter a sound.

When the retreat is coming to a close, break the silence with a
time of spoken prayer. Consider taking the Lord's Supper
together before you speak. Then spend some time allowing
people to share what God has done for them during their
time of silence.

Encourage each person to return home with a goal of creating
times of silence in his or her daily life. We live in an
overwhelmingly and increasingly noise-filled world. Silence is
a gift we give our soul and an opportunity we give our Lord.

As Theresa of Avila writes, "Settle yourself in solitude and you
will come upon Him in yourself."[19]

Learn to Function in Your Giftedness

When you became a Christian, the Holy Spirit was given to you, and
you were gifted with the presence and power of Jesus. Christians
are the continued presence and ministry of Jesus Christ in this world.
Do you know what God has gifted you to do? Learning to function in
your giftedness will simplify your life. Your spiritual gifts are the best
indicator of how God would have you spend your time in ministry.
When you serve using your gift(s), you can be the presence of Jesus
to those around you.

A spiritual gifts assessment may help you to discover how God
has gifted you for ministry. Set aside at least thirty minutes for this exer-
cise. Spend some time in prayer, seeking the leadership of the Holy
Spirit before you begin. Then prayerfully work through this inventory.

Your ministry is not limited to your gifts, but your choices are more
easily defined by knowing them. This inventory will help you understand

which part of "the body of Christ" God has created you to be. Your life will be simplified when you understand that not every need constitutes a call. You are only part of the body of Christ, and you are only accountable to God for what he has called you to accomplish.

SPIRITUAL GIFTS INVENTORY

Who has spiritual gifts?

Every believer has at least one spiritual gift (1 Corinthians 12:7, 11; Ephesians 4:7), given at his or her salvation. No believer has every spiritual gift (1 Corinthians 12:12, 27, 29-30). Our gifts differ from each other (Romans 12:3-6). We receive our gifts according to God's will, not our own desire or experience (1 Corinthians 12:11; Ephesians 4:7-8).

What are the spiritual gifts?

The New Testament includes three lists of spiritual gifts. In Romans 12:3-8 we encounter seven gifts:

prophecy
serving
teaching
encouraging
contributing to the needs of others
leadership
mercy

In 1 Corinthians 12:7-11 we find nine gifts:

wisdom
knowledge
faith
healing
miraculous powers
prophecy
distinguishing between spirits
speaking in different kinds of tongues
the interpretation of tongues

191

And in Ephesians 4:11 we discover five gifts:

apostles

prophets

evangelists

pastors

teachers (some interpreters see pastors and teachers as two
  separate gifts, though the Greek syntax seems to indicate
  that they are one function)

This gifts discovery tool does not include the so-called "sign"
gifts (healing, miracles, tongues, and interpretation of tongues),
although many believe they are valid today. Generally speaking, many
churches do not offer ministries utilizing them. The inventory includes
the additional gifts of music and hospitality since many interpreters
see them as spiritual gifts (see 1 Corinthians 14:26 and 1 Peter 4:9-
11), and because they are very important to most churches and their
ministries.

Combining the various lists, this gifts discovery tool catalogues
eighteen different gifts:

- **administration:** organizing people and ministries effectively
- **apostleship:** adapting to a different culture to share the
  gospel or do ministry
- **discernment:** distinguishing spiritual truth from error or heresy
- **evangelism:** sharing the gospel effectively and passionately
- **exhortation:** encouraging others as they follow Jesus
- **faith:** seeing God's plan and following it with passion
- **giving:** investing with unusual sacrifice and joy in God's
  Kingdom
- **hospitality:** using your home and/or resources to help others
  follow Jesus
- **intercession:** praying with unusual passion and effectiveness

- **knowledge:** discerning and sharing the deep truths of God's Word and will
- **leadership:** motivating and inspiring others to serve Jesus fully
- **mercy:** showing God's grace to hurting people with unusual passion
- **music:** sharing God's truth and love with unusual effectiveness
- **prophecy:** preaching the Word of God with personal passion and effectiveness
- **serving:** meeting practical needs with unusual sacrifice and joy
- **shepherding:** helping others grow spiritually
- **teaching:** explaining God's Word and truth with unusual effectiveness
- **wisdom:** relating biblical truth to practical life with great effectiveness

Some of these ministry areas are the responsibility only of those gifted to fulfill them, while others are the responsibility of all believers. For instance, those with the gift of prophecy should preach; those with the gift of teaching should teach the Bible to others; those with the gift of apostleship should be leaders in missions-oriented ministries.

On the other hand, God expects all of his people to discern truth from error, share their faith, encourage others, have faith in him, give sacrificially, show hospitality to others, intercede regularly, seek to know and share his Word, offer mercy to hurting people, meet practical needs with joy, help others grow spiritually, and relate his truth to life.

Whether we are gifted in these areas or not, we are responsible to meet these needs as God directs us. Those with spiritual gifts in these areas will typically be called to lead the rest of us in these ministries, and will model them with great effectiveness. Those who possess the gift of evangelism, for example, encourage us to share our faith when they demonstrate their gift in action. Those with the gift of serving will take the initiative to help in this area and will show the rest of us how to serve with joy.

The spiritual gifts do not confine our service only to the areas where we are gifted. Rather, they point the way to ministries where we can lead and serve with our greatest passion and joy.

What are my spiritual gifts?

The following assessment is based on the belief that our passions and opportunities indicate the spiritual gifts God has imparted to us. Our passions indicate those areas of service which correspond with our desires, abilities, and interests; we may or may not have used these passions in ministry to this point in our lives. Our opportunities show us areas where God may have opened doors of service to us, and may indicate areas of spiritual giftedness. This assessment will help guide you in the process of identifying these gifts.

Instructions: Read each statement and then rate yourself based on your perception as to how true each statement is about yourself.

5–Almost always true

4–Often true

3–Sometimes true

2–Seldom true

1–Almost never true

_____ 1. People often tell me that I am a good organizer of groups and committees.

_____ 2. Traveling and experiencing different cultures excites me.

_____ 3. When I hear a sermon or Bible study, I seem to be able to tell when the speaker is teaching God's Word and when he or she may be off track.

_____ 4. I get excited at the prospect of talking to someone about the gospel.

_____ 5. I look for ways to speak a positive word to people, especially when they are lonely or hurting.

_____ 6. I seem to be able to trust God in hard times, even when others struggle with their faith.

_____ 7. I enjoy contributing financially to the needs of others.

_____ 8. I love opening my home to others.

_____ 9. When I hear about a need or problem, my first response is usually to pray.

_____10. I seem to have a gift for understanding what the Bible means by what it says.

_____11. I find great joy in helping a group of people define and achieve their goals.

_____12. I especially enjoy helping underprivileged people.

_____13. I especially enjoy using my musical abilities to help people follow Jesus.

_____14. I find great joy in proclaiming the word of God in public.

_____15. I am happiest when I work behind the scenes.

_____16. I have a deep desire to help other people become fully devoted followers of Jesus.

_____17. I find great joy in teaching the Word of God to others.

_____18. When I read the Bible, I can usually tell how it relates to our problems today.

_____19. When I am part of a disorganized group, I become frustrated and want to help.

_____20. I seem to adapt to different languages and environments more easily than other people.

_____21. I am very concerned about helping people distinguish spiritual truth from error.

_____22. I look for opportunities to share the gospel with people.

_____23. I enjoy sending notes and cards to encourage people.

_____24. Others seem to be inspired by my strong faith.

_____25. I look for ways to invest my resources in the Kingdom of God.

_____26. I enjoy preparing meals and decorations to make a ministry event successful.

_____27. Spending significant time in prayer is a very important part of my ministry.

_____28. I especially enjoy studying the Bible and discovering its applications to life today.

_____29. I become frustrated when a group does not have a clear purpose and strategy.

_____30. My heart goes out to people who are suffering, and I want to do all I can to help them.

_____31. I am drawn to ministries which enable me to use my musical gifts for God.

_____32. I sense that the Holy Spirit gives me the ability to communicate his word clearly in public.

_____33. I don't seem to get as weary in doing tedious work as others.

_____34. I would be willing to invest a significant amount of time in helping a small group of people grow closer to God.

_____35. I sense that the Holy Spirit speaks through me to teach God's Word to others.

_____36. I seem to have a gift for finding biblical truth which meets the practical needs of others.

_____37. I can often see the end from the beginning and know what steps to take to accomplish a goal.

_____38. I get excited at the thought of living in a different culture for the purpose of helping people follow Jesus.

_____39. People often ask me to help them when they need to know the right thing to do.

_____40. I am willing to take personal risks for the sake of sharing the gospel with others.

_____41. I have a strong desire to counsel hurting people.

_____42. I can consistently see the purpose of God in the circumstances of my life.

_____43. I find great joy in knowing that my financial gifts will help other people follow Jesus.

_____44. I often invite people to my home and enjoy serving them there.

_____45. I find great joy in spending a significant amount of time in prayer.

_____46. Other people often ask me to help them understand the Bible.

_____47. When I become involved in a group, its members often ask me to lead.

_____48. I enjoy serving in hospitals, shelters, nursing homes, and benevolent ministries.

_____49. People tell me that my musical gifts help them worship God.

_____50. When I speak in public, I seem to have a gift for connecting God's word to the needs of those who listen to me.

_____51. I find joy in helping people meet their practical needs.

_____52. When I join a group, I feel responsible for helping the other members grow spiritually.

_____53. When I teach God's Word, I seem to have a gift for connecting biblical truth to the lives of those who listen to me.

_____54. In a group setting, others seem to look to me for counsel.

_____55. People often ask me to help organize groups and accomplish goals.

_____56. I would be willing to make personal sacrifices for the sake of reaching people in different countries.

_____57. My impressions of people's character and intentions are usually proven right.

_____58. When I share my faith with people, they often seem to respond positively.

_____59. People who have come to me for encouragement and comfort often tell me that I have helped them.

_____60. When I find myself in difficult circumstances, I welcome them as an opportunity to watch God work.

_____61. When I hear about a ministry opportunity, I get excited about the chance to contribute.

_____62. I see opening my home as a significant way I can help others follow Jesus.

_____63. People know of my personal commitment to prayer ministry and often call on me to pray for them.

_____64. I enjoy writing and sharing the insights I have gained from my personal Bible study.

_____65. I seem to have a gift for motivating and guiding groups of people to accomplish their goals.

_____66. I am deeply concerned for those who are going through hard times.

_____67. When I perform musically, I can sense that the Holy Spirit is using me.

_____68. When I proclaim God's word in public, people tell me that they hear God speak to them through me.

_____69. I feel that God wants me to help the church by meeting the practical and physical needs of others.

_____70. I am very concerned about the spiritual maturity of those I know.

_____71. People tell me that they hear God speak through me when I teach his Word.

_____72. When I have a problem, I can usually find the biblical wisdom I need.

_____73. I enjoy opportunities to use my organizational skills for God.

_____74. I am drawn to opportunities to serve God in a different culture.

_____75. I have learned to trust my intuition in knowing truth from falsehood.

_____76. I am able to share my faith very naturally and easily.

_____77. I am naturally able to find a way to comfort hurting people.

_____78. I am consistently confident that God's purpose will be fulfilled in my life and circumstances.

_____79. I am drawn to opportunities where my financial resources can make a difference.

_____80. I enjoy ministries which need help with hospitality.

_____81. I am excited about spending time in prayer with other people.

_____82. I am drawn to ministries which enable me to share biblical truths I have discovered.

_____83. When I lead a group, people affirm the effectiveness of my work.

_____84. When I am involved in benevolent ministry, people affirm the effectiveness of my work.

_____85. I find great joy in glorifying God through my musical abilities.

_____86. I am drawn to opportunities to speak God's word in public.

_____87. I enjoy serving God by meeting the routine needs of the church and her people.

_____88. I am drawn to groups of people whom I can help to grow spiritually.

_____89. I enjoy opportunities to teach God's Word to others.

_____90. I am drawn to opportunities to help people solve their problems by discovering the biblical truth they need.

Now finish your profile by putting your score in the corresponding box and then totaling each category.

Administration	Apostleship	Discernment	Evangelism	Exhortation
1.	2.	3.	4.	5.
19.	20.	21.	22.	23.
37.	38.	39.	40.	41.
55.	56.	57.	58.	59.
73.	74.	75.	76.	77.
Total:	Total:	Total:	Total:	Total:

Leadership	Mercy	Music	Prophecy	Serving
11.	12.	13.	14.	15.
29.	30.	31.	32.	33.
47.	48.	49.	50.	51.
65.	66.	67.	68.	69.
83.	84.	85.	86.	87.
Total:	Total:	Total:	Total:	Total:

This inventory was used with the permission of James C. Denison, www.godissues.com

Faith	Giving	Hospitality	Intercession	Knowledge
6.	7.	8.	9.	10.
24.	25.	26.	27.	28.
42.	43.	44.	45.	46.
60.	61.	62.	63.	64.
78.	79.	80.	81.	82.
Total:	Total:	Total:	Total:	Total:

Shepherding	Teaching	Wisdom
16.	17.	18.
34.	35.	36.
52.	53.	54.
70.	71.	72.
88.	89.	90.
Total:	Total:	Total:

Find the names of the gifts with the three highest numerical values. These are considered your primary gifts.

My Primary Gifts are:

1._____

2._____

3._____

Now that you have identified your primary gifts, look at some of the possible suggestions for using those gifts in the descriptions that follow. Add to the list as you discover more about the particular gift.

Administration: Consider the areas of ministry that require organization and advance planning. Retreats, banquets, and other gatherings often require staffing, publicity, and budgets. Volunteer your giftedness to such programs and know that you can help provide a time for people to spend some significant, often life-changing moments with God.

Apostleship: If you are someone who has a passion for those who are outside the walls of the church and desire to bring them in, consider creating avenues of ministry outside the church programs. You may volunteer in a community service organization or mission that provides food, counseling, or educational programs. When you are a friend to people outside the church, you may have the opportunity to tell them they also have a friend in Christ.

Discernment: Not everyone can tell when a ministry or messenger is Spirit led. Many things are done in the name of Christ, but not with Christ, under his leadership. Discernment is the ability to perceive the presence of God and his blessing on a ministry. Prayerfully and carefully help others to "be about the Father's business."

Evangelism: All Christians should share their faith with others, but there are some who are uniquely gifted to the task. Consider helping people to know how they can best share their faith with others. Look for opportunities to volunteer for ministries that reach out to a non-Christian audience.

Exhortation: There are always people who notice when someone needs encouragement or counsel and seem to know the right words for the moment. If this is your gift, live with a Spirit-led awareness and don't hesitate to write that note, make that phone call, or speak the words that God has laid on your heart. Your encouragement may make all the difference to someone and provide a source of strength for their life and ministry.

Faith: The person gifted in faith is often able to see the bigger picture and trust that God will provide. Every committee and every program needs someone who can voice the larger goals of God and encourage others to think and plan beyond their human limitations.

Giving: Those who have this gift are often blessed with the ability to provide materially or financially to a ministry. Those who give generously are often the reason a program or ministry is successful and accomplishes what God has intended. These people lead by example in the area of stewardship.

Hospitality: The ability to make someone feel at home when they are not is a great blessing. If people come to your home or into your presence and feel welcomed, then you have a wonderful gift. Consider volunteering your home for a Bible study or a church program. Chances are, if your home is a comfortable place to be, the people will be more open to all that is said and done for the Lord.

Intercession: The ability to pray for other people is the quiet gift of knowing how and when to lift the needs of others to the Father. The gift of intercession means that you have a passion for prayer and know the eternal significance of calling on God. Be a person who "prays without ceasing" and give your time and attention to the call of prayer for the people and programs of the church.

Knowledge: Those with the gift of knowledge are often those who give the "best answers" in a class or Bible study. If you understand the meaning of Scripture and its application to life, consider voicing your answers in class, respectfully keeping others on track with the intent of the passage. Some people with this gift teach in an up-front capacity, others teach quietly one-on-one. The joy is knowing that what you teach is the truth of God's Word.

Leadership: Those gifted in this area are not necessarily those who desire to lead, but those who just naturally have a following. The gift of leadership is found in those who cause others to follow. A gifted leader is the one who is committed to seeing a ministry project through and is willing to be responsible for its purpose. The key to being a gifted leader is recognizing the crucial need to follow God and help others to do the same.

Mercy: The gift of mercy is the gift of serving with compassion. Most Christians can offer mercy; those who are gifted offer the mercy of God to others. If you are filled with God's mercy for others, consider volunteering for those ministries that reach out to people who are in a crisis situation or who don't have a place to call home. The gift of mercy is to offer the love of God to others.

Music: Those gifted in this area have the ability to use their voice or musical ability to bring glory to God. Many people are able to perform a song, but the gift of music is the ability to use song to bring God glory and make him known to the listeners.

Prophecy: This is quite simply the gift of preaching God's word and will to others. The giftedness is that the "sermon" is not the message of the person speaking, but the ability to put aside his or her thoughts, and voice God's. A true prophet brings God's message, not his own.

Serving: The gift of serving is found in those people who never see a task and measure whether it is worthy of their time. Those gifted in this area are the people who meet the needs of others and the needs of the church with the quiet joy that comes from living as a blessing to others. All of us are called to serve, but those who are gifted are those who make themselves available to others for God's sake.

Shepherding: People gifted in this area are often those who lead Sunday school classes or other small groups. These are the people who know whom God has given them to care for and nurture. Shepherds invest their time in the lives of others and God gifts them to know how this can best be done.

Teaching: A gifted teacher has the ability to communicate the Word of God to others. One who is gifted can teach the lessons God intends for the day from the passage. If this is your gift, pray about who God wants you to teach and how he wants you to teach them.

Wisdom: Wisdom is the unique gift of knowing God and how he is at work. The gift extends beyond knowing what needs to be done, but how God would have it done. If you have the gift of wisdom, use it to help others know God and how they can serve him with their lives.

You're at the end of the book. What have you highlighted that you want to remember? What subjects do you feel you need to continue to study? What commitments do you know God wants you make? Someone once said, "One can always measure a man's devotion to the cause of Christ by his readiness to be called to responsibility, by his diligence in it, by the personal risks he runs through his involvement in it, or by the ease with which he lays it down."

Heavenly Father, strengthen us to fulfill our call. We want to be your devoted children, but it is so easy to rest in your grace. May we always remember that you lead us to a life of blessing. Forgive us when we choose not to follow. We love you, we trust you, and we are amazed you adopted us into your family. May we live godly lives, worthy of your name. Amen.

NOTES

1. Oswald Chambers, *My Utmost for His Highest*, rev. ed., ed. James Reimann (Grand Rapids, MI: Discovery House Publishers, 1992), March 17.
2. Martin H. Manser, ed., *The Westminster Collection of Christian Quotations* (Louisville, KY: Westminster John Knox Press, 2001), 144.
3. Ibid., 353.
4. John R. W. Stott, *Between Two Worlds: The Challenge of Preaching Today* (Grand Rapids, MI: William B. Eerdmans Publishing Company, 1982), 204.
5. Manser, *Westminster Collection*, 307.
6. Ibid., 319.
7. Ibid., 399.
8. Ibid., 68.
9. Ibid., 364.
10. Ibid., 254.
11. Ibid., 19.
12. Ibid., 376.
13. Ibid., 384.
14. Ibid., 362.
15. Ibid., 92.
16. Chambers, *My Utmost*, August 5.
17. Manser, *Westminster Collection*, 125.
18. Ibid., 363.
19. Ibid., 352.

For anyone who has ever wrestled
with life's disappointments . . .

there is something better within your grasp.

REFUSING TO SETTLE FOR LIFE AS USUAL

hoping for
something
better

a 10-week journey through the hope-filled message of Hebrews

NANCY GUTHRIE

Acclaimed author Nancy Guthrie has a message for those of us who yearn for more out of life but have trained ourselves to expect very little. Join her as she applies the ancient truths of Hebrews to our very real needs of today—the needs for significance, security, and hope for the future—and encourages us to refuse to settle for anything less than the something better we've been hoping for all along.

"God had planned
something better for us."
Hebrews 11:40

CP0119

Blessed

discovering God's
bigger dream
for you

B.L.E.S.S.E.D.

ROBYN HENK

What if God's idea of blessing is far more than we can ask or imagine?

If life is not what you dreamed it would be, it's time to be B.L.E.S.S.E.D.

Bible teacher Robyn Henk learned the secrets of God's blessing in the crucible of her own shattered dreams. Her story—and the scriptural lessons she shares along with it—will touch you at the point of your own dreams and draw you closer to God's heart. Along the way, you will find, as Robyn did, that letting go of human agendas allows God to work out his bigger, better dreams for blessing you.

CP0238